deliberate motherhood:

12 key powers of peace, purpose, order & joy

The Power of Moms

Published by The Power of Moms

Copyright © 2012 The Power of Moms

All rights reserved.

ISBN-13: 978-1479295852
ISBN-10: 147929585X

First edition 2012

Printed in the United States

Cover photo by Cary Brege

Cover design by Rebecca Walters - Merrakai.com

Visit us at www.powerofmoms.com/book

TABLE OF CONTENTS

PART FOUR: Joy

ACKNOWLEDGMENTS

Getting this book to publication has been a labor of love from our Power of Moms community. We give our deepest thanks to those who contributed to this project, as well as to the million plus mothers who visit our website and, most importantly, exemplify deliberate motherhood in their own homes and neighborhoods.

We sourced the content of this book from our very first Power of Moms Writing Contest in November of 2010, and we selected the incredible cover photo by Cary Brege from our April 2012 Photo Contest. We offer a huge thanks to *all* the mothers who participated in these contests.

We also want to thank our volunteer board members who performed the lion's share of the work on this book:

Alisha Gale, for receiving and organizing our 170+ writing contest submissions, coordinating the judging process, and continually jumping in to help where needed. And her husband, Jared, for contributing his legal expertise as we embarked on this project (which turned out to be much larger than expected).

Anna Jenkins, Rachelle Heyworth, Rachelle Price, Laurie Brooks, Melanie Vilburn, Mindy Thurston, Koni Smith, Megan Stewart, Amber Gillette, Mary Christensen, and Shawnie Sutorius, for working tirelessly alongside our 12 main authors to read each contest submission and help us decide which stories and ideas needed to be in this book.

Catherine Arveseth and Allyson Reynolds, for spending countless hours bringing our 12 unique chapters together for the first time and creating a cohesive message from more than 60 voices.

Linda Eyre, for inspiring all of us as mothers, writing the foreword, and being the mom to four of our authors.

Richard Eyre, for encouraging us each step of the way and championing this organization from the beginning.

Mindy Thurston, for coordinating hundreds of emails back and forth with our authors as we finalized the details of the publication.

Rebecca Walters, for volunteering her time and talents to design the *beautiful* cover.

The mother and her two children who posed for the cover photo, inspiring us to be more deliberate as we raise the next generation.

Chantól Sego, for happily taking on the massive assignment of putting together the whole book, including formatting, editing, and taking care of so many details.

Our wonderful Advisory Board, including Whitney Johnson (whitneyjohnson.com), Kelly King Anderson (startupprincess.com), Kathy Clayton, Margaret Archibald, Richard and Linda Eyre (valuesparenting.com and theeyres.com), and our wonderful husbands, Eric Perry and Jared Loosli, for their guidance, examples, and support.

And finally, we thank all of the family members who encouraged and supported us in this project . . . and provided the experiences from which we were able to write. Each idea, each story, and each "ah-ha" moment recorded in these pages was done solely with the intent to reach back and strengthen families who can benefit from the words of those who have gone before.

Love to all of you!

April Perry and Saren Eyre Loosli
Power of Moms Co-Directors

FOREWORD

THE HAND THAT ROCKS THE CRADLE
Linda Eyre

Perhaps "powerful" is not the first adjective that comes to mind when we think of motherhood and what it means in our day-to-day lives as moms. But motherhood is powerful beyond measure. Your influence as a mother is more exciting than you know and more long-lasting than you can conceive. While we can feel pretty powerless as the laundry piles up and the baby cries, we, as mothers, have amazing powers that can be defined and refined to yield beautiful results. With inspiration from the 60 mothers who contributed their stories and hard-won wisdom to this book, motherhood becomes more stimulating, more rewarding, and more deliberate.

In the late 1800s, William Ross Wallace wrote a beautiful poem about motherhood that includes this phrase at the end of each stanza: *"The hand that rocks the cradle is the hand that rules the world."* For good or for ill, mothers are shaping the next generation of children who will shape the future of our world (even though it might seem that they're only capable of making messes at present). Barbara Bush got it right when she stated at her Wellesley College Commencement address, *"Your success as a family, our success as a society, depends not on what happens in the White House, but on what happens in YOUR house."*

As a mom, what you do today and each ordinary day that follows with your children is more important and more dramatic than any of us can imagine. Through sometimes-tedious daily routines, we teach our children about love, tolerance, patience and understanding—just as surely as we teach them how to make snap judgments and how to get angry. (I know . . . I wrote a book when all our nine children were home called *I Didn't Plan to be a Witch*.) But as long as your children can see that you are valiantly trying, that you love them dearly, and that they are your first priority, great things will come out the other end!

Much of what you are teaching your children today will also seep through the generations to your grandchildren and great-grandchildren and on and on. I love this quote by Anna Quindlen:

"We are building for the centuries. We are building character, and tradition, and values, which meander like a river into the distance and out of our sight, but on and on and on. [Motherhood] is a way of life, chosen in great ignorance and the bedrock of much of what we are, and will become."

As we focus on nurturing our children and helping them become the people they need to be, we can and should focus on nurturing the various "powers" that reside within *us*. Personal development does not need to happen at the expense of our children's development. In fact, our children's development *depends* upon our personal development. The refiner's fire of motherhood changes you. It can make you better. We can truly become the people we really want to be through striving to become the mothers we really want to be.

The outstanding authors of this book have let the trials and hardships of motherhood make them into better people. Whether the change includes learning patience when the two-year-old "paints" your walls with the black permanent marker or forgiving a teenager who screams "I hate you," or loving *more* when that naughty child doesn't really deserve it, it's a change that *refines* us— or as the dictionary describes it, "removes impurities, makes something more effective or become more elegant." That is powerful!

You may think that everything has been said about motherhood, but the delightful thing about this book is that every mother/author is one-of-a-kind. They each come from different backgrounds, have different parents, are married (or not) to different people, and certainly have "different" children.

Each of the 12 "Powers" expanded upon in this book is a crucial component to help you in your motherhood. And the best part is that you don't need to do it all at once. You can focus on one "power" a month, and over the course of a year, you'll see great changes in yourself and in your family. The mark of a great book is that it makes you think . . . and it helps you change . . . which in the case of this book, is an absolute guarantee!

INTRODUCTION

by April Perry and Saren Eyre Loosli
Co-Directors of The Power of Moms

Remember the first time you held that beautiful little bundle and set off into the wide world of motherhood? Did you feel excited? Did you feel scared? Did you wish your little bundle came with an instruction manual?

There can't possibly be an instruction book that covers every situation you're going to experience as a mother. Could anyone have foreseen the seven minutes you spent peeling Band-aids out of the inside of the dryer, the two hours hopelessly trying to get Vaseline out of the carpet, or the three months nursing ear infections? Then, of course, there were those six months dealing with non-stop squabbles between two of your children (who simply didn't seem to like each other), and the good part of a year spent comforting your pre-teen daughter who felt like no one liked her.

Motherhood can definitely be tricky, but it's not just our interactions with our *children* that leave us searching for answers. It's our experiences refining *ourselves*.

Many people ask us what we mean by "Deliberate Motherhood." In our opinion, it means that you really think about what you do as a mom. You really care about your family and want the best for them. Plus you want to learn and grow and develop yourself as a person through the experience of motherhood. You live life purposefully. You embrace what you uniquely bring to your family.

When we take on the title of "Mother," that doesn't displace our personhood. Now we simply have more facets, and we need to make some critical decisions. What *kinds* of mothers do we want to be? What kinds of people do we want to be? Can we develop our unique talents and fulfill our own needs while being great mothers? Can we create amazing families while simultaneously thriving as women?

Being deliberate is about having it all (but not necessarily all at once). It's about using the very experiences of motherhood to develop the people we are inside—and finding greater fulfillment and joy in the process.

Each mother's situation is unique because each family is unique, but through the 12 years we've each spent as mothers and through learning from the moms we've met in person and online through running our website for the past 5 years, we've come to believe that there are some basic, fundamental principles of happy, meaningful motherhood.

To identify and explore these principles, we gathered some of the best mom-writers we know and asked them to help us clarify what it is, exactly, that helps mothers feel more in love with their families while experiencing more of the progress and fulfillment that motherhood can offer.

We came up with 12 core principles (or "powers," as we like to call them), and they make up the basis of the 12 chapters in this book—grouped additionally into four categories: Peace, Purpose, Order, and Joy.

Each chapter features the voice of one main author and several supplemental authors chosen from our Power of Moms Writing Contest. You'll notice that some chapters have one main essay with supplemental pieces at the end, while others weave all the voices together into a united whole. Either way, the result is powerful.

And when these 12 featured powers are examined, understood and applied, they change our lives. What you'll read in this book is the proof.

How to Use This Book:

One of the most exciting things about this journey you're about to take is that you don't have to do it alone! This book serves as the curriculum for the Learning Circles program on our website, which gives you the tools to meet monthly (in person or virtually) with a small group of like-minded mothers and focus on one power each month. (We've spelled out all the details at www.powerofmoms.com/book.)

So read the book as your personal self-study course in becoming the mom you really want to be. Or read it with friends as part of a Learning Circle. Either way, the stories and poignant thoughts in this book will get you laughing, thinking, and figuring out your own personal path towards the powers that will bring you more peace, purpose, order and joy in your life.

Motherhood is wonderful. Motherhood is worth the effort. Motherhood will shape and transform us into women with strength and character that far exceeds our current expectations.

We're excited to grow with you. Welcome!

PEACE

Allyson Reynolds, a Midwest girl, met a California boy in Japan and married him quick. After living in both Iowa City and Los Angeles, they've finally settled in the mountain west with their four endearing children.

After participating in the first-ever *Power of Moms* board meeting (attendance 3!), Allyson's been hooked on doing whatever she can to strengthen mothers. This enthusiasm has led to various speaking opportunities, including those at The Power of Moms Retreats. Her speaking material comes largely from the stuff she writes for the website and as director of the *Motherhood Matters* blog. Before motherhood became her greatest teacher, Allyson earned a B.A. in family science.

In a parallel universe, Allyson travels the world as a freelance writer and National Geographic photographer. In reality, she tries to squeeze in as many of her favorite things as possible (her family, the great outdoors, photography, blogging, riding her bike, cooking, living like a tourist) in between treating stains and signing school papers. She blogs at allysonreynolds.blogspot.com.

CHAPTER ONE

BEND WITH IT
The Power of Acceptance

by Allyson Reynolds

"Good timber does not grow with ease; the stronger the wind, the stronger the trees." J. Marriott

I can still see myself sitting there, swollen feet propped up on the camel-colored recliner we picked up at a garage sale, with a pile of books stacked up next to me: every 'baby bible" on pregnancy, childbirth, nursing, and the first year of life. I would spend hours during that first pregnancy reading those books with the naive hope that it would ensure my success as a mother. I was going to be the best mom.

The only problem was, I didn't count on my baby having a hard time learning to latch on, or anticipate the difficulty of functioning under the fog of chronic sleep deprivation, or doing everything on my own as my husband worked over a hundred hours a week, or the frustration of trying to be cute and stylish on a really tight budget with a flabby postpartum body. And I certainly didn't count on my baby turning into a teenager. There wasn't anything in those baby bibles about teenagers.

My own mother was the quintessential homemaker. She sewed matching 70's style prairie dresses for me and my sisters, made homemade wheat bread for my brown bag lunch, and served up

3

both green and orange vegetables for supper from her own garden. My childhood memories are full of fresh-smelling sheets, snuggling up for reading time on the couch, and singing around the piano. After this upbringing, motherhood should have come much more easily. I should have been a natural.

Looking back, I realize that maybe I *was* a natural—as natural as a new mother could be. But I was a sapling, wanting to be an oak tree overnight. And maybe I wasn't even an oak tree at all! Maybe I was a willow, or an ash, or a pine. (Some women *do* seem better suited to carry the burdens of motherhood.) No matter, I was a sapling, trying to push back a self-loathing for all the supposed inadequacies and imperfections of my "mother self" who had barely begun to emerge.

I desperately wanted to be a "good mother." I had imagined myself in a rocking chair, singing sweetly to a newborn as she drifted off to sleep (in my beautifully-decorated nursery), my husband playing happily with the children in the next room while I peacefully made dinner (in my well-stocked and immaculately-clean kitchen), gathering my brood around me to read books together at the end of the day (on my stylish couch next to the fireplace), or taking my well-behaved and neatly-groomed children on stimulating outings (trim, toned, and stylish myself).

But I didn't feel like a good mother at all. A good mother doesn't wake up with a feeling of dread or anxiety about being left alone all day with her baby and toddler. A good mother doesn't go to bed with the house in shambles, let her children watch TV so she can have a minute to herself, serve frozen pizza for dinner, or any of the other myriad offenses I committed on more than one occasion.

And I admit it: I didn't always like being *the mom*. I mean, I *loved* my children, but I didn't always like the work associated with being their mother. And don't good mothers love what they do? Wasn't it exactly what I had signed up for? The definition of the verb "to mother" is to nurture, protect, and care for, but what that actually looked like on an ordinary day was vastly different from the visions I had nurtured for so many years.

What was all this endless whining, crying, mess-making, disciplining, shopping, coaxing, budgeting, negotiating, laundering, calendaring, cooking, cleaning, and the constant feeling I was always forgetting something?

My list of annoyances and inadequacies seemed as endless as my misery. What was wrong with me? Where was the joy? The growth? The fulfillment I was so certain I would find in this, the most important job on planet earth—that of raising another human being to adulthood?

If only I could go back in time, I would love to tell my sapling-self a few things. Things I have long since dealt with and embraced as truth. Things that now bring me comfort and strength instead of frustration and discouragement. Things about acceptance.

Accept that Motherhood is Hard

Real hard. If motherhood were supposed to be easy, it wouldn't be so hard. (How many ways can I say this?) As a teenager, I read M. Scott Peck's book, *The Road Less Traveled*, and his words have saved me time and time again—especially as a mother:

> "Life is difficult. This is the great truth, one of the greatest truths. It is a great truth because once we truly see this truth, we transcend it. Once we truly know that life is difficult—once we truly understand and accept it—then life is no longer difficult. Because once it is accepted, the fact that life is difficult no longer matters."

From the sleepless nights and physical stress of the infant and toddler years, to the sleepless nights and emotional stress of the teen years, motherhood demands *a lot* from us. That truth isn't going to change anytime soon, so we may as well own it. Acceptance is the point at which motherhood becomes easier—accepting that it isn't getting any easier.

Accept that There's No Such Thing as "Done"

This is an extension of accepting that motherhood is hard, because part of what makes it so hard is the never-ending nature of a mother's work. I always chuckle a little sarcastically when I hear myself say the dinner/laundry/bills/homework/shopping are done. Whoever heard of such a thing? It's as silly as saying the children are done!

Stop trying to get to "done"—to an imaginary finish line at which you can finally stop, stand still, and say "I did it!" Yes, there are markers and milestones, times when you can take stock and feel a sense of satisfaction, but by and large, motherhood is not a project with an end point.

Accept Yourself—Warts and All

It's hard to move forward with your life and accept the other people around you if you're not at peace with yourself. Accepting ourselves as we are is often hindered by what I call "The Compare Snare"—comparing our weaknesses against other people's strengths. Most notably, other mothers. Imagine for a moment a world without blogs, home shows, or parenting/decorating/ fashion magazines. How would your life be different? Of course it's nice to get ideas and inspiration from outside sources, but how often do you go from getting ideas and inspiration to comparing, coveting, and coming to the conclusion that you just don't match up?

Do yourself a favor: throw 'em out and turn 'em off. At least minimize their influence. Becoming the best mother you can be is about learning to follow your own inner compass, not somebody else's. The sooner you can learn to accept and appreciate yourself for who you are, the sooner you can start living with a greater measure of peace and contentment.

There is also comfort in knowing that our children are blissfully ignorant of our so-called inadequacies—they think we're perfect just the way we are (at least until they're teenagers . . .). They don't see our cellulite, our deflated bank accounts, our cluttered closets, let alone our undeserved self-loathing. All they see is their mother; the woman who takes care of them, feeds them, hugs them, listens to them, *loves* them. When you inevitably feel unqualified for the task at hand (and we've all been there) remind yourself that motherhood is ultimately about your children, and they think you are wonderful!

Accept Imperfection

About those warts. Why do we try so hard to make our lives appear "perfect" when in fact it is the imperfection that perfects us? The child with an illness or disability that teaches us how to really pray and sacrifice; the difficult teenager who pushes us to dig deeper and love more; the "daily grind" that forces us to get more organized and disciplined; the financial struggles that keep us humble and motivate us to reach out to others struggling in similar ways. You see?

Anna Quindlen shared these words of wisdom: "The thing that is really hard, and really amazing, is giving up on being perfect and beginning the work of becoming yourself." The irony of that statement is that if you do 'become yourself,' you *will* be perfect, for you will be who you were created to become. It helps me to think of the word 'perfect' as a verb, rather than a noun. To perfect means to improve, refine, hone, work on. Instead of trying to cover up the messiness of motherhood, embrace your perfectly imperfect life and let it work its magic!

Accept that Your Best Really is Good Enough

Can you accept that even on your worst of days and in the worst of circumstances, your best really is good enough? We tell our children this all the time, but do we afford ourselves the same kindness? It would be nice if every day was like a scene out of Mary Poppins, but you know what? We haven't died and gone to heaven yet, and as mentioned before, motherhood is hard. Even if you cry, lose it when you're frustrated, and give up on occasion (only to get back up again), that doesn't mean you're a failure. It means you're a mother.

And why, oh why, when the going gets tough do we add insult to injury by mentally ripping ourselves to shreds? What *is* our obsession with negative self-talk? Much like our children, we need nurturing to grow into our best selves, but we'll never get there if we spend our days saying things to ourselves we would never dream of saying to our children. Would you want your daughter to talk to herself the way you talk to yourself? It doesn't do you or your children any good, so kill the inner critic and be kind to yourself. And encouraging. And complimentary. And forgiving. And supportive. (Doesn't that feel better already?)

Accept Your Current Stage of Motherhood

Being an empty nester probably sounds the most attractive when you have a house full of small children, and having a house full of small children probably sounds the most attractive when you're an empty nester. Every stage of motherhood has its challenges and blessings, and the worst mistake a new mother can make is to think "it will get easier when . . ." or "I'll be happy when. . . ." It may get

8

easier in some ways, but you can count on it getting more difficult in others.

I recently found myself in the most adorable boutique and bistro you've ever seen. Shabby chic and chocked to the brim with the most beautiful baubles and trifles a woman could ever hope to grace her home/wrist/hair. I took my three daughters there on a whim, in between a trip to the post office and the grocery store. *Just a little look-see and cupcakes*, I told myself, because a place like that isn't really meant for small children. I was feeling that familiar feeling: suppression of my annoyance at their desire to touch every blessed thing, to talk too loud, to ask for too much. Oh, how I wished to come to a place like this alone, to buy what I pleased, and with money that wasn't already called for! And then I saw it: the sign.

"Kiss your life. Accept it just as it is. Today. Now. So that those moments of happiness you are waiting for do not pass you by. Kiss your life today. Now. Just as it is."

I've never appreciated a good slap in the face more than I did at that moment.

Accept Your Reality—Both of Them

Today you may carry the burden of single motherhood, or have a rebellious teenager that wants to engage you in daily arguments. Maybe you don't have enough money to fund all the lessons, activities, and family vacations you always dreamed of, or you shudder at the sight of your postpartum body. Perhaps you are exhausted from caring for a sick or disabled child, or you struggle with secondary infertility, postpartum depression, or—heaven forbid—all of the above!

Most of us could come up with a long and detailed list of all the injustices life has thrown our way, and we may be correct in our assessment, but there is still another reality—a parallel reality, if you will. What is yours? Today, mine is a healthy body for the day's work, a little naked bum running down the hall, narcissus blooming on my kitchen counter, the sound of laughter, a friend for my teenager, inspiring music, and having loved ones who love me back.

Acceptance is not about throwing your hands up in the air and surrendering; it is about making peace with the bitter, as well as embracing the sweet. We create our own reality by choosing what we see. See the sweetness! See the joy, the beauty, and the tender mercies in your life as a mother. You can spend your precious time and energy wishing away your circumstances, wishing you had so and so's "perfect" life, but the reality is, happiness does not come from having what you want, but by wanting what you already have.

Remember the description of my idyllic childhood? Could it be possible that amidst all the cookie-baking, homemade costumes, and euphoria of childhood that my own mother struggled just as I struggle now? Of course she did. My own "quintessential" mother and homemaker suffered many challenges, disappointments and heartaches over the years. No mother gets through unscathed—it's almost a guarantee. It may take several children and decades of time, but eventually "life" catches up to most of us. Still, she was a giant of a mother, and I never knew any differently.

Accept the Struggling that Makes Us Strong

Why do we think we are weak because we struggle, when in fact it is in the struggling that we become strong? Yes, if I could go back in time, I would tell my sapling-self that it's not the type of tree you are that matters. What matters is how we build our root systems to stand up to the wind and how we use that wind to make ourselves stronger. It's the trees with the strongest root systems that endure the mightiest winds, by bending and flexing under their pressure.

Accept the wind. Face it, open to it, bend with it, and be grateful for it. It is turning you into the mother you are meant to be.

****

The Perfect Body

I was surprised to look down during church today and see, folded neatly in my lap, my mother's hands. I remember sitting next to her in church, looking at her hands and thinking how old they looked. Now those old hands are mine—complete with club thumb!

I feel some pressure from society to be horrified by the fact that I don't look as young as I used to, but today I don't. As I sat looking at my hands, I thought of all that they accomplish. Just like my mother, and her mother, and her mother before that, these hands have done a lot of work.

They have washed dishes, scrubbed floors, changed *many* diapers, wiped away tears, and applied band-aids. It is only right that they are looking older and well worn. They've earned that!

I think about the rest of me, too. The slowly deepening creases on my face have their own stories to tell. Those lines mean that I have smiled much, and cared enough to worry sometimes. There are marks left by the sun, and some left by times of stress. And then there are my stretch marks—a constant reminder that I have born and nurtured many children.

In spite of the aesthetic imperfections, I am in awe of what a gift my body is to me.

It is strong enough to work hard, to love, to serve and to care for my family. It has enough flaws to provide me with trials and opportunities to grow. It somehow knows how to create beautiful little bodies for my children. What a miracle is the gift of life!

It is my body. And it is perfect just as it is.

- Christi Alston Davis

The Swing

I love to see my husband on the swing
that hovers soft across our porch out front
with Madeleine on one thigh cradled close
and Lily on the other. Early on,
before the sonogram, he wanted sons
and now he has two daughters, both with chins
that dimple like his own, and eyes shot through
with chocolate brown, like his, my favorite brown.
He points out passing cars and lizards in the hedge.
He sings *Mi gallo se murió ayer*
in silky baritone, the Spanish smooth.
Enrapt, they listen, daddy's voice a song
unparalleled, a music sweet as memory
of heaven. Nothing rivals what I see:
a cord of love as strong as that which binds
my girls to me.

- **Dayna Patterson**

Good Mom Redefined

Did you know?

- "Good moms" don't choose to ignore their children, and there are times I do just that. I lie in the bathtub and read my book while my boys scream and argue. "Good moms" (if taking a bath at all) would promptly exit the tub and happily deal with the situation. Sometimes I don't. Sometimes I even shut the door to muffle the sounds of chaos.

- "Good moms" don't resent the time their children take away from them. I do. Can't they see I'm having "me" time? Can't they see I am *busy?* Please, do not ask for apple juice, snacks, or a video right now.

- "Good moms" don't snap or yell at their children. Not when they are tired, or on the phone with the electric company, or trying to have an adult conversation with one of their few remaining friends. "Good moms" always talk nicely to their children.

- "Good moms" do not feel guilty about what they *should* be doing or what they *could* have done because "good moms" have nothing to be ashamed of or feel guilty about.

My four-year-old was following his usual pattern. Getting out the door had become a battle, and by the time all of us were in the car, my frustration and anger were boiling over. Although I tried to contain it, my anger overflowed, and I behaved badly. I yelled at my children, banished the barking dog to the backyard, and snapped at my husband. It wasn't pretty, and I knew that at the end of the day my husband would want to talk.

I was not in a good place to have that conversation! I ranted and downloaded every detail of my day concluding that *clearly* it was my poor mothering skills that had caused the day's chaos. I confessed my sins (as listed above) and then I said it: "Maybe I'm not a good mom."

As the words came, a huge weight lifted from my shoulders. I felt free. A large grin appeared on my face, and I couldn't stop it. I wasn't sure why I was reacting this way, but I felt good! It was the beginning of realizing that my rigid definition of a "good mom" was unfair. I had set myself up for guilt, shame, and failure. My definition of a "good mom" did not allow room for *me,* and who I am.

As I begin to contemplate a new, more flexible idea of what it means to be a "good mom," I am embracing the thought that maybe I can still be a good mom and raise good kids even when I occasionally do something "bad!"

- Kim Dettmer

Heaven Around Me

On the night of December 31, 2006, my three children and I were driving home from my parents' house when my then seven-year-old daughter, Olivia, looked beyond the seat in front of her to the valley ahead. "The world is a treasure box, and the lights of the city are the treasures!" she exclaimed.

That same night, my five-year-old son, Isaac, prayed sincerely to have a really good dream about eating a life-sized chocolate egg. And Grace, my three-year-old, asked me again if I would *please* change her middle name from Emma to Alyson. Their typical expressions of children were also expressions of hope in their newly-uncertain world.

As 2007 began to settle upon me the next day, I reflected upon the difficulty of the year behind me, and hesitated as I considered the year ahead. I solemnly recognized that I was not going to be the mother I had been in the past. I was not even hopeful about becoming the mother I imagined in the future. I was only capable of being the mother I could be in that moment—single, working, and attempting to create a life beyond survival.

With all my focus on not drowning, I had forgotten my strength, both in my body and my mind. And failed to identify the life preserver floating right next to me. I noticed it for the first time and took hold, letting the waves of acceptance crash around me. I felt peace, as I gave up all the unnecessary flailing. My New Year's gift to myself.

Sometimes I feel I am being tossed upon a sea, a raging tempest of obstacles surrounding me, barely able to catch air at times. And yet, the storm occasionally calms just enough for me to catch a glimpse of the horizon ahead. The view is not crystal clear, but it is visible enough to keep me moving forward. My sweet children are my jewels, like the city lights of Olivia's perfect world, or the stars that seem to stare down upon us like angels and protectors during the lonely nights.

I do not have the power to stop life, but I have the power to breathe and let life go ahead of me for a moment. I can resist and risk drowning in the storm, or I can let the waves cleanse me and move me forward. There is always a choice, and anything but acceptance will surely lead to greater hardship and loss.

I accept these treasures, this journey, this view. I accept whatever it is I can give right now.

Olivia once said, "It feels like we are in a dream, and if we're real good, we'll wake up in heaven." I hope I will wake up every day recognizing the heaven that is around me right now.

- Mary Anne Stewart

The Reality of Me

By Hollywood's standards, I will never be skinny. My legs will always be short, my knees always chubby. My body will forever be a testament of motherhood—a little softer, a little looser, a little something more to suck in.

Me.

I am not a photographer. Sometimes I catch great moments with my little point and shoot, but they are only great because of the subjects I'm capturing, not because I know how to do anything beyond, well, pointing and shooting.

I am not a chef. I can manage meals for my family that make them happy and keep us fed. But to me, it's just cooking. Passionless. Obligatory.

I am not a musician. I can stumble my way through a few pieces on the piano—flawed, fumbled, tolerable, at best.

I am not an artist. I am stick figures. I am third grade trees.

Sometimes, I'm short tempered. I jump to conclusions. I think I know everything. Sometimes, I fail to see.

Me?

This is me.

I'm a curvy, comfortable size 10 and I own my body.

I'm a good mother, a good listener, a good friend. I can speak in public. I can make beautiful quilts. I'm a good runner, a powerful swimmer.

I am a writer.

And you know what? I like this person that I am.

In this skin, in these jeans, I am comfortable.

Sometimes though, I slip. I hesitate to embrace the reality of me and instead look at what others are, what others can do.

I compare.

And then I shake some sense into myself and remember that comparisons aren't fair to anyone. What a disservice to someone's talent to only enjoy it through a veil of jealousy, to waste time that could be spent appreciating and enjoying by tearing myself down over something that I am not, that I may not ever be.

I remember that when I love who I am, it is much easier to love others for who they are.

When I love me, I can marvel at brilliant pictures I didn't take, and revel in delicious meals I didn't cook. I can listen to lovely music and appreciate the talent of those that are performing. I can notice how great someone looks in a size 6. I can admire and respect others for their gifts, knowing that it has nothing to do with me, that it takes nothing away from what *I* can do.

So today, everyday, I embrace me, for all that I am… and all that I am not.

- Jenny Proctor

Making A Trade

I grew up fantasizing I would have it all. I would meet "him," he and I would fall madly in love, marry, have babies, raise them, and gracefully grow old together. I would float around in expensive silk shirts and perfectly-placed hair, gadgets swinging open in my spotless kitchen, kids sitting in a perfect row waiting patiently for me to toss fresh baked cookies into their hands.

Well, I met "him," and he was perfect. We were perfect. (You think "perfect" when you're head over heels.) Before I knew it, we were married and I was moving in.

He was divorced and had a daughter, so as soon as the ring was placed on my finger, I became an instant mother figure in our home. My husband's work schedule changed to weekends three days before our wedding. It was in his daughter's best interest to keep a steady school schedule, so she was with "us" on the weekends. This meant that I not only became an instant mother figure, but I was also flying solo. I quickly found out that being a mom was hard. Having a mothering role without being the actual mother was even harder.

There was one night in particular the two of us came down with something. I didn't know what to do. I called the one person I knew could help me—my own mother. After talking to her and then tending to my step-daughter, I went to my room, slumped onto my bed, and cried. I was awful at this. I knew that I represented a huge change for this little girl. I was trying so hard to fight the step-mom stigma—too hard. I felt she was comparing me to her mother. I felt judged and alone. And I became afraid: afraid to add pieces of me to our home, to share my own traditions and style and quirks.

That first year brought the natural ups and downs of life—miscarriages, financial struggles, schedule changes, and eventually a successful, but very hard pregnancy. I didn't float like that woman I had envisioned (I was lucky if my dishes were done). Instead I learned to surrender and be okay with that. This wasn't my ideal back when I was dreaming of "him," but I wouldn't trade him or his little girl for anything. I traded my attitude instead. I stopped focusing on how things should be or could be, and began to accept things as they were.

- **Heather Doyle**

The Inner Cheerleader

Recently, my five-year-old daughter, Lexi, helped me unload the dishwasher. Because she was working like such a busy little bee, I said, "Lexi, you sure are a great worker!" She looked up at me, grinning with delight and self-satisfaction, and then broke out into song: "I am a great worker! I am a great worker!" She repeated this about 25 times, and then finished it off with, "And I am a great person!!"

It was refreshing for me to see that little girl so confident and pleased with herself. There was no self-doubt, no false modesty, just joy in who she truly was. I wished in that moment she would stay like that forever.

When was the last time you told yourself you were a great worker, or even a great person? On the other hand, when was the last time you scolded or criticized your self? Self-acceptance, peace, and gratitude will spread like a warm blanket over your entire family when you quiet the inner critic and replace her with an inner cheerleader.

- Shawnie Sutorius

Good Enough

After a long day of dishes, laundry, and managing our family's schedule, my head sinks into my pillow as I see in my mind a young woman from years ago. She sits in a rocking chair, dressed only in a robe, hair pressed against her head, limp and wet. Tears fall silently down her cheeks as she fixes an empty stare on the snuggly pink blanket that drapes gently across her arms, her new little bundle wrapped securely inside. The dark, sunken circles surrounding this woman's eyes suggest a sleepless night, and the heaviness of her expression suggests a weight she does not yet know how to bear.

I search beyond her expression and explore her thoughts. She is trapped somewhere in the middle of her blissful, nostalgic past and the suffocating, frightful present. Throwing her head back and resting it on the pillow at the top of the chair, she recalls the lively days, just weeks earlier, when completing assignments, preparing for meetings, and gathering with co-workers for short breaks in the cafeteria consumed much of her life. She longs to return to that familiar routine and to the feeling of confidence that came from years of experience, lots of mistakes, and plenty of training. The little one cries out, forcing the woman to engage in the moment. She attempts a various number of tricks to try to placate her disturbed child for the longest stretch of time possible. Wanting to break down, but knowing it would be pointless, the woman seeks for some clarity.

The role of mother had been worked out in her head long before her little one was born. In her imaginations, motherhood was blissful. The events of her days were in control, peaceful; she loved her life. Instead, the reality of her situation feels far from those dreamy ideas of her creation.

In her soul, she knows she must love this child, yet she isn't certain she is prepared to accept the changes that must take place in her life to shoulder such a trusted responsibility. She feels like a stranger in her own life, her feet transferring warily from bed to floor each morning onto unfamiliar territory. Prepared or not, she begins her new role in an entry-level position. She is as a character in a play—acting out someone else's life as she moves toward the whimpering sounds in the next room. She is unsure of how she will comfort her little one, but is determined to try.

~ ~ ~

The clock chimes in the other room. I roll over, once again finding my favorite pillow spot. I'm wide awake now, and I stare out my window into the dark night. I ponder the differences between my life back then and my life now—two lives that seem worlds away from each other.

Back then, I did everything I thought I *should* do. I did the things I thought would make me feel and look like a good mom. I took

loads of photos, scrapbooked every nook and cranny of my baby's life (even though I dreaded the hobby), and nursed until my mutilated nipples bled and nearly detached from my breasts. I stuck to a solid routine (meal time, play time, nap time), then did it all over again two or three times until bed. I spent every waking minute of my baby's life interacting with her on the floor.
I didn't know how many more repeats of *Itsy Bitsy Spider* and stackable cups I'd be able to manage. I didn't know how many more well-balanced meals I could prepare for baby when all that was calling to me was chocolate, potato chips, and ice cream. I didn't know how many more diaper blowouts it would take to finally suppress the gross-out factor I experienced each and every time.

Even if anything I was doing made me *look* like a good mom, I didn't *feel* like much of anything. I looked forward to nap time, and kind of dreaded wake-up time. I thought freedom would never come for me again. And I yearned for kindergarten!

Something was missing, but I didn't know how to fill in the holes. As time passed and two more daughters joined our family, I became more comfortable and familiar with the day-to-day life of a mom. I also slowly started to let go of guilt-ridden, self-imposed obligations. After years of engaging in a hobby that didn't interest me, the scrapbooking supplies were finally boxed up for good. After years of being the entertainment committee and schedule planner, my girls were given the opportunity to entertain themselves alone in their room for periods of time each day called "quiet time." And after years of doing anything I could to calm them down, I finally realized that I wasn't a bad mom if my kids were sometimes left alone to cry.

Although I'm still resistant to change and not as flexible as I would like to be, I am a different mom than I was ten years ago. I'm different today because I have a different attitude toward parenting. Where I once sought to control, now I seek to influence. Where I once thought I should intuitively have all the answers, I now realize I am still learning and ask for help when I get stuck. And where I once cared how others viewed me in my role, now I parent for my children and not the approval of other people.

There was a time when I felt like I was suffocating. I was unsure of whether or not I would ever feel good enough as a mom, or whether or not I would be as good of a mom as someone else. Those days are gone.

Today, I know I'm a good mom. Not because I am always a consistent and gentle disciplinarian when behaviors around my house are less than acceptable. Not because I serve a vegetable at every meal. Not because I keep my composure under the most stressful of circumstances. And certainly not because I perfectly fulfill all the hopes and expectations my children have of their mother—or that I have of myself! No. I can't say that I do any of these things.

Today, I know I'm a good mom because I am committed to my children and to myself in this role. I know I am a good mom because I respect my children and realize they have a great many things to teach me. I know I am a good mom because I get out of bed every single morning, even on the days when I would rather be free to wander and forget for a while that I am tied to responsibilities. I know I am a good mom because I follow my heart and do the things that feel right for me and my family.

And for today, that's good enough.

- **Rachelle Szymanksi**

Saydi Eyre Shumway grew up in London and Salt Lake City as the fourth of the nine children of best-selling parenting authors, Richard and Linda Eyre. She went east for college and grad school (Wellesley College and Columbia University), and met her husband Jeff while working in DC. They've lived in the Boston area ever since. After earning an MS in social work, Saydi worked with disadvantaged expectant mothers for many years.

While she fondly remembers extensive travel and adventures across Africa and Asia during her growing up and single years, Saydi's latest big adventures have included a trip to Target with four peevish children to see what kind of diapers are on sale. Saydi loves running (especially when it doesn't involve running after her kids) and is also a professional photographer in her precious spare time. She blogs at bostonshumways.blogspot.com.

CHAPTER TWO

PUT YOUR HEART ON
The Power of Love

by Saydi Shumway

I am constantly *doing* for my family. Mostly I'm doing things out of love, but I doubt my children always feel loved as I frantically move them through our daily routines. It's homework, dinner, chores, potty, hands, teeth, pajamas, book, prayer, song and bed. I breathe a big sigh of relief once I finally get those bedroom doors closed without further protests.

Then eventually, after I finish cleaning the kitchen, folding laundry and paying bills, I sneak into their dark rooms to cover them up. There they lie, angelic and heavy with sleep. In those quiet moments, without the busyness of life cluttering things up, I always feel that powerful mother-love well up inside me.

I remember the funny things they said and did during the day that I was too distracted to stop and savor. I think of the promises I made but never kept. That book I never read or that new Lego creation I never looked at. As I watch them sleep and reflect on the day behind us, I get a little glimpse of their world, how hard it is to navigate and how much they need the security of my love wrapped around them.

I stand by their beds and squeeze their little hands or stroke their foreheads or press a kiss hard on their cheeks in an attempt to stamp their little beings with all the love I was too preoccupied to dish out during the day.

I can empathize with this mom's story:

> *My four-year-old daughter and I have a little ritual we do together when I really need her to listen to me. We call it "putting your ears on." Before I tell her my important information, I ask her to put her listening ears on, and she pretends to grab imaginary ears and put them on. It works wonders! But, as motherhood often goes, this little trick of mine sort of backfired one day when I was reminded how wonderfully clever our children can be.*
>
> *This same four-year-old was howling in the backseat of our minivan. Although she had just eaten her ice cream cone, she wanted her little brother to give her some of his. I tried reasoning with her, but I guess I wasn't being particularly empathetic. Finally she said in her most serious tone, "Mom! I think you just need to put your heart on!"*
>
> *- Danielle Monson*

Love is the most powerful force we have as mothers, yet how often do we move through our days without putting our hearts on—forgetting to feel and express the love that really is at the core of all we do?

Love and Affection is Every Child's Most Basic Need

After graduating from high school, my courageous and crazy parents packed us up—me and my six siblings who were still living at home—and we flew to Romania to volunteer for one month in an orphanage. Following the reign of Ceauşescu, who banned birth control in hopes of building a bigger and stronger empire, Romania exploded with children. Mothers who were unable to care for their children were forced to hand them over to institutions with the hope that they would at least get fed. The children did get fed, but because the institutions were so overcrowded and understaffed, they were not held or nurtured.

When we arrived at our little orphanage, we spent the entire day trying to satisfy one desire. The children wanted to be lifted up and held. They screeched, "Sus! Sus!" (Romanian for "Up! Up!") over and over as they ran up to us. We would pick them up, one by one, squeeze them tight for a second, then put them down, and they'd scramble to the end of the line where they would wait patiently for their turn to be lifted up again.

They were desperate to be held and touched and loved—even for a second. Touch was something most of them had lived their entire lives without—something they were starving for. Many of them had not been born with any physical or mental problems, but they were suffering from developmental and physical delays simply due to a lack of individual attention and love.

Love is critical to child development. Study after study links proper brain function and development to touch, love and affection. Children adopted from institutions where they have had adequate attention and affection, but severely inadequate physical nourishment and medical attention, often recover quickly with a few months of infant formula and the care of a good pediatrician. In contrast, infants who have spent significant time in institutions where they have been emotionally neglected, but physically cared for, can take years, if not a lifetime, to recover from the trauma.

In the 1920s, New York pediatrician, Dr. Henry Chapin, reported an alarming death rate in children under two who were placed in institutions across the United States that provided adequate food and shelter, but no emotional nurturing. Dr. Chapin concluded that children need to be held, carried and caressed in order to not only develop properly, but to survive.

Neurologists have found that love and affection fosters brain development by releasing hormones essential to building proper neurological connections.

In his book, *Biology of Love*, neurologist Dr. Arthur Janov states, "Hugs and kisses during critical periods [of child development] make neurons grow and connect properly with other neurons." Essentially he says that you can "kiss [a child's brain] into maturity." Love can affect brain development and behavior right up through the teenage years. Children and teens who lack proper touch, love and affection show significantly decreased attention span, decreased self esteem, problems with addiction and an impaired ability to relate to others and navigate loving relationships into adulthood.

All these studies, statistics and thoughts about love and its immense power knock around in my head as I think about my job as a mom. I feel the weight of my children's need to feel love. Not just any love, but *my* love. How well am I loving my children? How can I more deliberately put to use the powerful force of my unconditional "mother love"? The kind of love that will give them strong brains and emotional intelligence, and help them feel secure and happy. Love that will enable them to go into the wide world and wield their own powerful love for good.

Recognize the Love that Motivates Your Mothering

With four small children it's easy for me to focus on getting things done rather than on loving. Love is not "productive." I can't check "loving" off my to-do list. Because love is process-driven and impossible to measure, loving doesn't even make it onto my list.

At its core, mothering is motivated by love. By recognizing love as the explicit motivator behind what we do, everyday, mundane tasks suddenly become meaningful. There are whole seasons of my life as a mom where I've forgotten this and have lived as if motherhood were about getting laundry done, or putting healthy meals on the table, or having a clean house, or making sure the kids are in the right schools. Sure, all these things are important, but only if they are rooted in love, and only if my family feels loved as I do them.

This year, after our traditional Christmas Eve dinner, I was pregnant and exhausted and frustrated by the seemingly impossible tasks that all need to happen at once on that 'magical' night. My sciatic nerve was shooting pains down my leg and more than anything, I wanted to just sit down and enjoy the tree and the fire.

As I went around slamming things into place, putting toys together, wrapping the last lingering presents, cleaning up and prepping for breakfast the next morning, it hit me that my attitude was preventing me from feeling the love that actually motivated the work I was doing. I was feeling resentment rather than love towards my family as I made my way through my work.

I realized that, for weeks, I had been resenting my children because they were in the way of all the things I had to do to pull Christmas off. I needed to flip my thought process and recognize that my love for my children and family was in fact the reason for all these tasks.

This was a big epiphany for me. My never-ending lists of things to get done won't go away until my kids are long gone. But if I can go about these tasks recognizing the love that motivates them, the spaces that were filled with bitterness and resentment can instead fill up with a powerful and compelling love.

Love Changes You

The magic of this realization is that when we perform our mothering duties with love, rather than resentment, the power of that love changes, shapes, and molds us—as much as it changes, shapes, and molds our children.

One mother relates her experience of how love can alter us and enable us to cope with difficult situations.

> *My two-year-old son is just like all other children. He gets frustrated. He gets mad. He gets angry. He gets sad. He gets fed up. He gets tired.*
>
> *When I feel myself running out of patience with him, and I don't know any other way to help him, I take him in my arms, hug him as tight as I can, and tell him I love him.*
>
> *Hugging him and telling him I love him doesn't usually make much of a difference in him. It does not stop the tantrum. It does not end the frustration. It does not make everything all right.*
>
> *Hugging him and telling him I love him makes a difference in me. It renews my patience. It makes me thankful for the moment and thankful for my son, tantrums and all.*
>
> *- Jenni Ellis*

Since becoming a mother I have been surprised by how profoundly my mother love has changed me. Surrendering to all that is involved in motherhood, even the mundane parts, and learning to daily acknowledge the love that is at the core of it all, has given me strength to do things I didn't think I could do. It has drawn out parts of my soul I didn't know existed. It has transformed the way I look at the world, deepened my empathy for others and refined my sensitivities. It has altered the way I experience life.

Loving Takes Effort and Planning

In his book, *The Road Less Traveled*, M. Scott Peck sheds light on what love is, what love isn't, and how we can use real love to powerfully alter our lives and relationships. He says, "Love is not a feeling. Love is an action, an activity. . . . Genuine love implies commitment and the exercise of wisdom. . . . Love is the will to extend oneself for the purpose of nurturing one's own or another's spiritual growth." These words ring true to me—real love takes effort, planning, wisdom, and commitment.

I confess, I dish out a lot more planning, effort, wisdom, and commitment to getting my kids fed and clothed than I do to getting my kids loved. In order to love our children well, we need to take time to sit down and think. We need to have a plan. What do we need to do more of? Less of? How can we ensure that "loving" is a daily "must-do" in our lives?

Learn Each Child's Love Language

Each child is different. Each needs to be loved in vastly different ways, and it takes effort and wisdom to figure out how to do that. I love this experience related by one mom.

> *In the book, "The Five Love Languages," author Gary Chapman suggests that we all need to be shown love in a way we recognize and that suits our individual needs. This is ever so true for children; they need love expressed to them in ways they understand. Chapman's "love languages" include physical touch, words of affirmation, acts of service, quality time, and gifts.*

31

My daughter and I went through a time when love just wasn't being communicated correctly on my end. She was three years old, and whenever I would try and teach her to behave, she would respond through tears of, "You don't like me mommy!" or "You are so mean!" Some days I'd think to myself, "Surely I have the skills to get along with a toddler!"

Our turning point came when I decided to devote part of my day to losing myself in play with her. I remember mustering up all of my enthusiasm so she felt like I was having the time of my life as we played endlessly with her dollhouse. It's hard for me to admit that playing with my children takes such a conscious choice (some of you moms are naturally so good at this). That day playing with my daughter was me, choosing to love.

As the day came to a close and my husband came home from work, my daughter went racing out of her room to enthusiastically say to her daddy, "Mommy and I are playing dolls!" He expressed his delight in her happy news, and then she said, "Yes, when I was little I didn't love my mommy, but now I love her so much!"

I was stung.

What did she mean she didn't love me? That is quite possibly the worst thing a mother can hear! Yet suddenly, I understood what my daughter was trying to say. She was telling her dad that I had just done something that made her feel loved. I was instantly so grateful I had learned that valuable lesson and had recognized a tool with which to love my child even better.

- Danielle Monson

As mothers, we need to learn to speak the love languages that our children speak. This is not an easy task. It requires real analysis, thoughtful discussions with our parenting partners, meditation, trial and error, and sometimes doing things for and with our children that we don't particularly enjoy. It's up to us to be the "love" experts and to 'speak' love to our kids in a way that will sink right down to their core.

Make Loving Our Families Part of Our Routine

We must build love into our lives. In her book, *I Love You Rituals,* Becky A. Baily makes a compelling argument that building a relationship in which your children feel loved above all else is key to raising smart, adjusted, and happy children. She suggests that one way to make sure your children feel loved is to build "Love Rituals" into your daily routines. Love Rituals are things you do deliberately and routinely that help your children feel your love. They are motivated only by the desire to connect and be with your children. I love the idea of building slices of time into your days and weeks where really loving your child is the only thing you're trying to accomplish—nothing else. Essentially, it puts "loving" on your to do list.

For me, the only way love rituals have really stuck is if I plan them to coincide with other already-scheduled parts of my life, if they are genuine, and if they fit my personality as well as my children's needs. A foot massage for Hazel after her Sunday morning bath, a lunch date after a yearly physical for each child, a silly tickle with Charlie at bedtime, greeting Emmeline's little toes with a kiss each morning as I take off her footy sleepers. Love rituals can be serious or silly, active and crazy, or soft and cuddly. But since touch is so important to children feeling secure, love rituals should often involve touch.

The beauty of love rituals is that they can be simple and take little time. To this day, when it's time to say goodbye to my dad after a visit, he looks deep into my eyes for a full five seconds—like he's looking right into my soul. He's done this since I was a teenager. It is his way of acknowledging that he sees, cares, and knows who I really am. Although it is a little strange, it makes me feel his love. It only takes five seconds.

Other love rituals might take a little more time, but they can be attached to things you're already doing. Let love creep into the spaces that are often filled with busyness and distraction. A friend told me that one of her best memories of her childhood was the 15 minutes after she got home from school each day. Her mom gave her and her siblings their after school snacks and just sat with them while they ate. No agenda, homework, cooking, or cleaning. It was just an available mom and something yummy to eat. I'm sure there were times that this didn't actually happen—times when babies were crying and times when my friend didn't really want to sit and be with her mom. But I love that she doesn't think about those times. What she remembers is the feeling that sunk into her through this routine expression of love.

As this mom expresses below, I have found that a good bedtime love ritual is key to my children feeling loved, rather than begrudged, as I struggle to put them to bed.

I have heard many parents speak fondly of bedtime; sadly, none of those parents were me. Bedtime at our house was filled with frantic, last-minute requests for water and snacks, songs and stories, and pretty much anything that kept them out of their beds for a few more minutes. I found I liked my children the least at the end of the day.

One evening, I was struck with inspiration. I told my girls that as soon as they climbed into their beds, I would tell them a secret. Giggling, they dove under their covers. I leaned over one little girl and spoke softly in her ear. I told her what I noticed that she had done well that day. The look on her face was thoughtful. Then I hugged her and told her I loved her and how grateful I was that she was part of our family. I did the same with her sister in the other bed. Not only did this quiet them down and get them in bed, but I could see they felt loved and valued. This meant much more than the usual, "I love you. Goodnight." They knew I loved them, and they knew one reason why.

- Shawnie Sutorius

I love the way this mother recognizes and describes the magical role that love rituals play in her family:

I come from four generations of women who are mild mannered and easygoing. I am navigating new territory as the mother of three spirited boys who never cease to surprise me with their competitive natures and strong wills. They learn and grow through passionate bursts of energy. While my boys wield foam swords in imaginative play, I dream of procuring a magic wand which will transform our emotionally charged interactions into bonding moments and bridge our differences in temperament. I've yearned for a fairy godmother to say magic words to restore the peace.

Fortunately, I have found magic without the appearance of a wand. It comes when I engage my children with simple expressions of love—special traditions for expressing our love that create peace and harmony in our relationships.

Often, these rituals surface spontaneously. On countless occasions when my son Clayton sees I am weary or frazzled, he will catch my eye, point from his eyes to mine and sign "I love you" with three fingers up and two bent down. My grumpiness fades as my heart melts. Other times, I have signaled in the same way to a son through a window, across a crowded playground, while he waits to perform in a recital, or while he runs the bases in a ball game. This simple gesture, uniquely ours, strengthens our bond and communicates love.

Other rituals are sprinkled into our daily routines. Before we part each morning, we huddle together and each child clamors for his turn in the "mush pot." Each is squeezed in a tight hug and emerges amidst "I love yous" knowing they are a special component of our family.

The best opportunities to build love into our relationships come when I tune into individual needs in the moment and provide personalized attention. Making a favorite snack, leaving a love note on a bed, recognizing a small accomplishment, discussing the details of a cloudy sky together, and spending special time doing an activity of my child's choice are all meaningful expressions of my love.

Someday my children will no longer request a lullaby or rush to be in the "mush pot." However, while our traditions of expressing love might evolve as we grow, their power to bridge our differences and strengthen our bond will not change.

- Laurie Brooks

Because the whole family—not just individual relationships with mom and dad—can provide children with a powerful source of security and unconditional love, love rituals can be designed to include everyone in the family. Family traditions around birthdays and holidays help children feel a sense of pride and belonging and can cast a powerful net of love over children that will help them navigate their world.

Love rituals can come in all kinds of shapes and sizes. We need to find the ones that will speak to us and to our children. In my experience, this means trying on a bunch of different love rituals. Some have felt pretty cheesy and unauthentic. My kids have even laughed at some of the things I've tried and can tell that they don't exactly come from my heart. When we land on one that feels right, I try to embrace it and work hard to make it happen regularly. It takes extra effort, but I'm convinced it is through these rituals that love gets written into our relationships, and I can't think of anything I could possibly put on my to-do list that would be more important.

When the Going Gets Tough, Love Harder

My oldest daughter is *different* from me in hard ways and *similar* to me in hard ways. At times our relationship gets tangled into knots and because we're both so darn hard headed, it's tough for either of us to untangle—to see our way back to neutral, loving ground.

A few summers ago, I was at the end of my rope. I was venting to a friend about how lost I felt and how worried I was that I was destroying my daughter and our relationship by my inability to react the right way. She said something I hope I never forget. She told me there had been many times when she had felt at her wits end with one of her children, and her answer was always to just love them more. Instead of strategizing about ways to help them behave, implementing new discipline techniques, or finding new ways to react to tense situations, she focused solely on dishing them out an extra large serving of love. She told me this strategy has never failed.

Since then I've tried it. And I have to say that although it's a simple strategy, it can be extremely hard to implement. I've found when I'm entrenched in a difficult mothering situation, it takes great humility and effort to show forth that extra bit of love. But when I can do it, even if it feels a bit contrived at first, it works like magic. It changes us both. I begin to fill up with real, genuine love, which drastically changes the way I view my children and helps me see clearly what they really need. And as my love miraculously softens them, melting away tension, we build solid ground that makes the rough times ahead easier to navigate.

I recently read about Parent-Child Interaction Therapy (PCIT), a type of therapy that has been used to help parents who have been abusive towards their children. The first step in the therapeutic process is for parents to spend five minutes each day in "child-directed" interaction with their children. During these five minutes, parents are to do nothing but be with their children on their children's terms. Because it can be surprisingly difficult to interact with your children on their terms, parents are coached through those five minutes by a therapist using sneaky little earpieces and a two-way mirror.

At first, most parents smirk at the suggestion that five minutes a day will strengthen their relationships with their children. However, research findings show that teaching parents how to engage with their children in child-directed interaction, along with teaching them skills to better recognize and praise their children, can drastically reduce the incidence of abuse. This kind of intervention has proven to be far more effective than simply enrolling the parents in anger management courses. Essentially, these parents are taught the art of actively loving their children in a way their children can recognize, and it changes things. It's fascinating to me that the answer to these severe parenting dilemmas rests in training parents how to practice real, hands-on love.

This mom gets it right: "When the going gets tough, love harder." Below she relates a few experiences that have proven the effectiveness of love in dealing with difficult parenting situations.

My parents are a great example of loving through hard times. When my sister was in her freshman year of college, her life turned upside down with the news that she was pregnant. She and my parents had dealt with some difficult things throughout her high school years. Just when things were finally looking up, she had to turn to my parents and bear the heart-rending news. She fully expected anger, lectures, and guilt-ridden words to follow her announcement. What took place instead was a small miracle for our family. My dad later said that as he took a moment in prayer to know what to say to his daughter, he had an overwhelming feeling that his only job was to love her. The time for strong words and lectures was over; his only responsibility now, as her father, was to express his love. I truly believe this experience was the catalyst in changing my sister's life. To be unexpectedly enveloped with love, even when you don't feel like you deserve it, is powerful.

I am inspired by the quote by Elizabeth Kubler-Ross, "I have never met a person whose greatest need was anything other than real, unconditional love. You can find it in a simple act of kindness toward someone who needs help. There is no mistaking love. You feel it in your heart. It is the common fiber of life, the flame that heats our soul, energizes our spirit and supplies passion to our lives."

My son was a perfect one-year-old (wink, wink) except for one little problem: he had a serious issue with biting. Oh, the agony I felt as I witnessed my sweet little boy bite and hurt other children. I had some serious low points, like the day my friend showed me five massive welts on her little boy's back caused by the teeth of my child. And then there was the day he got written up at my gym's daycare for "provoking violence" and "failure to obey the rules!" You walk away from those little moments thinking everyone must think you are a terrible mom.

Luckily, I received advice from some women that I treasure, and I was told to simply love him. Love, love, love him, and then love him some more (all the while being rigidly consistent with teaching him the right way). I realized this phase would only last a minute in the grand scheme of things, but the way I was handling the situation with my son could set a precedence that would be lasting.

I can safely say my now two-year-old son has improved dramatically. And it's funny, but having gone through that trying stage with him makes me love him all the more because we loved our way through something tough.

- Danielle Monson

Love can solve a multitude of problems. It can cover up our mistakes. It can make us resilient. It is the strongest antidote to our most serious dilemmas as mothers. While it won't always magically fix or change everything, it will fix and change us.

Love Spreads

As I watched my little Hazel, all grown up, march into school for her first day of kindergarten, I felt my throat tighten. Would she like her teacher? Would she make friends? Would she feel secure? Does she know who she is? Does she know how much I love her? What will she share with the world? What have I etched into her heart?

Like every mom, I want my children to leave my home equipped with all the tools that they need to be happy and contribute to the world in a positive way. But more than anything, I want my children to go out into the wide world knowing how to love—how to truly, deeply and completely love others.

Every way we love our children teaches them how to love others. Our love will one day pass through them and spill out into a whole new sphere.

If we watch, we can see evidence of our love spreading through them and onto others. The following story demonstrates how beautifully our love can come full circle.

It was a beautiful springtime day—one with that Zip-a-dee-doo-dah kind of feel, but of course, it was the one day I became unusually sick. Moms aren't supposed to get sick, but if it does happen, what do we end up doing? We work right through it, right? As mothers, we keep pressing forward—it's in our genes.

We know no one is going to spoon-feed us Chicken and Star Soup, no one is going to put little wet towels on our forehead, and no one is going to kiss our rosy little cheeks and tell us, "Don't worry, you'll feel better soon." It's one thing to be sick, but it's another when you're the only adult at home with a husband away on business. What can you do?

On this particular day, I was so sick I really couldn't work through it anymore. I just rested in bed, head throbbing, fever running, body shaking—and I felt miserable. I said a little prayer hoping that someone would call to see how I was doing. I said another little prayer that someone might stop by to help me out. I even tried calling a friend, but all I got was her answering machine. I was miserable and saw no relief in sight, so I just kept on praying.

As my eyes began to swell with tears, who should come up to see me but my little ten-year-old daughter, Maddie? She saw that I didn't look very well, so she gave me a big hug and then asked if I was feeling okay because I felt really hot. I told her I didn't feel very well and that I just wanted to rest. She gave me a hug and then slowly left the room.

After a few minutes had passed, I heard a little knock on the door. Maddie came in with little wooden tray that contained a book to read, a Capri Sun, a handful of Goldfish crackers, and a peanut butter and jelly sandwich. She covered me up with her favorite blanket, tucking it under my legs, just the way she likes me to do it for her. It made my heart melt. Who knew that tucking a blanket under your legs when you were sick made your temperature drop by five degrees?

I gave Maddie a big hug and thanked her for taking care of me. She told me that I always take care of her, so now she was going to take care of me. My heart and my eyes began to overflow with tears of love for her. It's just so wonderful to see how love can be displayed by the smallest of gestures—even by the smallest in stature.

- Lisa Hawkins

Love spreads, and through loving our children, we are weaving threads of love into the fabric of the world.

When We are Present and Uncluttered, We Let Love In

"Our lives are frittered away by detail ... simplify, simplify."
– Henry David Thoreau

Life is busy. As a mom it is frightfully easy to let our days be frittered away by details, only realizing as we fall into bed at night that we didn't really live the day. We were moving, certainly moving, but we weren't present. Love happens in the present and is hidden in the moments.

My youngest sister, Charity, has had a lot of vicarious mothering experience. As the youngest of nine siblings and the only sister yet to have kids, she is our go-to girl when any of us need some extended child care in order to travel or work. I love her fresh perspective on what it means to mother and why we do it day in and day out. Sometimes when you're in the trenches you don't see things quite as clearly. These are her words:

> *I spent the past week babysitting my brother's three small children. I am a seeker of all kinds of adventures, and this was one like no other: a glimpse into the trump-all adventure of parenthood.*
>
> *Among other things, I kissed owies better, tried to sooth choruses of screams when I really felt like screaming myself, changed the world's most epic stinky diaper (you are probably thinking, "I have seen worse," but I honestly doubt it), drove to the elementary school in my nightgown, made a memory game and a chalkboard canvas out of the driveway, wiped up literally countless piles of spit-up, barely won the wrestling match in the pew during church, safely (but perhaps just barely) frequented the swimming pool and the school playground, sang lullabies, made pigtails, shook formula into bottles and desperately promised fruit snacks for good behavior.*
>
> *Every night when the kids went to sleep at 7:30, I was exhausted. It was fun, but there were flashes when the thought, "I really can't do this!" ran through my head.*
>
> *Here is the naive and amazed question of my childlessness—how do parents do it?*
>
> *I found the answer in a tiny flake of split-second bliss where I felt what I'm sure is just a small taste of a certain brand of golden, liquid joy preserved for moms and dads. It was an*

emotion that would absolutely propel a parent to keep going, week in and week out, no matter how crazy things got. It was a simple moment, but miraculously and magnificently energizing, empowering, motivating and so, so, so beautiful.

I was sitting on the beach. The sun was saying goodnight with simple yellows and the lightest of blues. McKay was digging, silhouetted in front of the shimmering waves, Baby Cubby was sitting nuzzled to my left side, and Lyla stood in the sand holding my thumbs—her feet willowed into the beach as she giggled in the amber light. Her hair was wispy and golden. Cubby's body was warm. McKay radiated the plain happiness of childhood. The hairs on my arms stood on end. The world stopped spinning. Just for a moment, just for that wildly beautiful moment, as if it was unable to contain the euphoria of such love.

Soon came the whines and the spit-up and the encroaching night. That beautiful moment didn't last, but maybe it will last me until I have a similar but amplified experience with a child that is mine.

I thank heaven that God has put into us this extraordinary but so human ability to love.

- Charity Eyre

Motherhood is hard. It is often the overwhelming love buried in small moments that "propels" us to keep going and going. The trick is to be present and uncluttered enough to see these moments—to let them fall into our laps. When we can grasp them and take them in, our love grows, our joy swells, and we are renewed.

When I analyze the times I'm unhappy as a mother, I find they always coincide with days and weeks and months when

I've overcrowded my life. Times when I'm overcommitted, times when my brain is overburdened by compulsions or discontent, and I'm distracted. When I can muster the energy and discipline to build in some space, un-clutter my life, and simplify things, suddenly I can see the crystals in the air, hear the music of my life, and drink in the present in all its glory. I can see the love that is laced through all I do. I can feel the power of mother love wash over me, push me forward, and fill up my family.

Love Will Exit the Other Side

"Love is the only thing that will exit out the other side. It will stand alone, vindicated. It will finally and clearly be seen for the dominant, unbeatable, infinite, glorified force it has always been, just obscured for millennia by layers of fallen clutter."
- Richard A. Swenson, M. D.

I want to be able to watch my sleeping children at night— assured they have felt the love that propelled us through the day. I want to "put my heart on" and wear it so boldly that they can't escape its powerful pull.

Our children will be gone in a blink. The difficult questions, the bad phases, the tantrums, the rebellions and our never-ending lists of things we want to get done will all come and go. But what will stand in the end is how well we loved.

Five children in four years, including two sets of twins, was a surprising life twist for Catherine after wading through years of infertility. Taking care of so many small children has been a challenge, but she and her husband, Doug, see their family explosion as an absolute miracle, a dream come true.

Catherine is the oldest of six children and lauds her parents for teaching her the importance of hard work and family. Two things that seem inseparable. She has a degree in Exercise Physiology, a minor in Creative Writing, is part of Segullah's Prose Editorial Board, and writes for Meridian Magazine.

She finds a busy family life most rewarding when she focuses on building relationships, laughing easily, cultivating gratitude, and choosing joy. Motherhood has turned her into a night owl, simply to preserve a sense of self and sanity (and keep the laundry moving). When not washing something or someone, she loves running the local canyon, reading, writing, and makes a mean dish of home-made mac and cheese. She lives in Salt Lake City and blogs at wildnprecious.com.

CHAPTER THREE

A DEEP BREATH
The Power of Patience

by Catherine Arveseth

A thin light limps through the kitchen window. I lean over the sink, searching for the sun as it flickers in and out of a hazed and swollen sky.

Tired, but determined to make a real dinner for my family, I bend over the counter and knead a sticky ball of dough. My boys are hungry—I can hear it in their cries. Spencer toddles into the kitchen, throws his arms around my leg, and wails into my pants. Gordon yanks on my apron ties and whimpers softly.

I sigh and keep kneading. If I were Elastigirl I could stand right here and reach that baking sheet in the cupboard over there. But I'm not, so I lurch across the kitchen with Spencer slung round my leg like a koala bear and Gordon impatiently cracking the reins to his newfound pony. I retrieve the baking sheet only to turn around and bump into Gordon who falls flat on his back. He hollers loud as I ease him onto my shoulder and whisper, "I'm sorry."

I call for my girls. No answer. I call louder and then raise a suspicious eyebrow.

We have five children five and under: a five-year-old daughter, three-year-old twin girls, and one-year-old twin boys. Any mother can imagine the state of glorified chaos that reigns under our roof.

Life is wild and busy; unpredictable but precious. Sometimes the bounty of it is so abundant I want to stretch the moment long, cup the joy tight. Other times I want to hand over my apron and make a run for it—anywhere. The evening hours are the hardest. My patience wears thin, little ones rumble restless and almost anything can happen.

With an awkward lift, I hoist Spencer onto my other hip and set off to find the girls. They are in the playroom swapping princess shoes and arguing over purses. I'm not in the mood to mediate conflict, so I leave them to their own peace-making skills, set the boys down with some matchbox cars, and return to the kitchen to finish dinner. Lifting the lid of the crock-pot, I check the carrots to make sure they're soft. They're not. And neither is the celery. Apparently, the low setting wasn't adequate and my soup has done nothing but mull for the last four hours. I scan the refrigerator for plan B, but my husband has been working late nights and these days, getting to the grocery store is like getting to the moon for me. We're pretty much out of food.

I open two boxes of macaroni and cheese and put some water on to boil.

Suddenly, a little warning bell goes off in my head. Check on the boys. I hustle downstairs. No boys. But I hear chortles and splashing coming from down the hall. I know exactly where they are. Someone forgot to close the bathroom door and they are crowded around the toilet. Gordon is plunging a Care Bear into the bowl while Spencer scoops handfuls of yellow water into his mouth. Not only did someone forget to close the door, they forgot to flush. I am horrified and both boys are completely soaked.

After stripping down the boys and cleaning up the mess, I am greeted at the top of the stairs by a lovely web of pink and purple ribbon strung from doorknob to doorknob. Two spools of my best ribbon have been spun out to the cardboard. I follow the trail to the couch and peer over the edge to find three girls huddled in a corner, each with a pair of scissors, snipping ribbon into confetti that now litters the living room floor.

"Really? This is my life?" I say out loud. The girls' eyes grow wide and the scissors stop.

I'm about to unleash a fireball of verbal frustration that has been building, and then I pause.

Deep breath. Walk away for a minute. You can handle this. . . .

Patience Defined

After our first set of twins was born I found myself saying, "I used to be a patient person. I used to be nice. I was calm, collected, and patient. What happened to me?"

Well, the reality is, I had kids. Let me explain.

Wikipedia defines patience as "the state of endurance under difficult circumstances, which can mean persevering in the face of delay or provocation without acting on annoyance/anger in a negative way; exhibiting forbearance when under strain, especially when faced with longer-term difficulties."

Those words most definitely describe the series of events above. I was delayed, provoked, annoyed, angered, and under strain. Before children, very few things provoked me. Sure, there was the traffic of Northern Virginia, the pressures of full-time work, our long struggle with infertility. But nothing compared to this.

Nothing compared to the maniacal mix of two inconsolable babies, not enough hands, four in diapers, endless potty messes, a box of saltines scattered indiscriminately around the house, lotion-lathered hair, "swimming" on the kitchen table (a recent favorite), entire rolls of toilet paper shredded behind closed doors, the laundry room "spot-treated" by two trigger happy twins, and running late because I have five free-spirited children to wrangle into car seats. Motherhood parachuted me right into the middle of a patience proving ground, and sometimes it feels like a war zone.

Cato defined patience as the greatest of all virtues and for good reason. Until we come face to face with circumstances that challenge our patience, it remains untried, untested, and under-developed. Patience is a process. It is discovered as we use it, much like a muscle. Overloading a muscle will stimulate the adaptive processes of the body. Just as that muscle will eventually be able to cope with the new demands placed on it, we too will find ways to cope with certain life situations, but not until the load presents itself. The defining question, however, is, "How will we cope?"

Several months ago I saw this quote on my friend's refrigerator:

"Peace - It does not mean to be in a place where there is no noise, trouble, or hard work. It means to be in the midst of these things and still be calm in your heart."
- Unknown

I decided then that I wanted that kind of peace. It may not be an isolated beach on Maui with a glass of mango juice and my favorite book. Those things would be nice, but I needed something now, some kind of eye in the storm—a way to be "calm in my heart" amid the chaos.

I knew patience was key.

Patience doesn't simply appear when we need it. It must be cultivated. I have learned a lot about myself (good and bad) since being pushed out of the chopper and dropped into the war zone. I've done some experimenting with patience, and here is what I've learned.

Give in Without Giving Up

Accepting that things are going to be hard is the first step. Adjusting mentally to a new plan, rather than feeling frustrated that things aren't easier, is the best way to begin.

"Always fall in with what you're asked to accept. Take what is given, and make it over your way. My aim in life has always been to hold my own with whatever's going. Not against: with." - Robert Frost

At some point or another, all of us will be required to accept something hard.

I have a friend whose husband is deployed overseas for months, sometimes a year, at a time. I have another friend who has four sons and recently went through a crushing divorce, which required her to return to work and move out of a home she loved. I know a mother who struggles to get up each morning and make her children breakfast because the pain of a stillbirth burns in her womb. I've seen the anxiety both husband and wife have felt after losing their source of income. I've watched families grieve the loss of a child or spouse, while others care for children with special needs—needs that require increased attention, doctors' visits, special therapists or schools.

Life doles out circumstances that not only make for difficult moments and days, but difficult years. Moving with what has been handed us, rather than against it, is the mark of graceful living— especially when faced with long-term challenges.

Somehow, just giving in to our fast and furious family life has helped me feel more patient with myself and others. It doesn't mean throwing in the towel and crying in a corner, tempting as that is some days. It means re-evaluating and adjusting my expectations so that they are reasonable.

After our boys were born, I lived most days in my pajamas only to realize at bedtime that I hadn't even brushed my teeth! My expectations were minimal: feed my children and feed myself.

Acceptance means finding a positive way to cope with the load we have to shoulder. It means acknowledging (but not dwelling on) the fact that the future is going to be difficult. It is knowing what Robert Frost knew. We can "make it over [our] way."

Know Your Triggers

When I lose patience, I feel bothered and defeated—like circumstance teamed up with my lesser self and won. So I've been trying to recognize why and when I feel impatient.

The process has been revealing. There are times of day I am more likely to unravel—certain situations or personal states of being that find me functioning with a shorter fuse.

Some triggers I can control. Others I can't. I can go to bed earlier. I can make sure I eat when my children eat. I can build larger margins into our schedule so we can get places on time. I can work on being more patient during the evening hours when I'm tired and going it alone. I may have to call on some deep reserves, but I can do it. Recognizing, anticipating and working to minimize triggers has set me up for more successful moments.

No day (or mother) is perfect, but self-assessment can help us improve.

Slow Down

Being in a hurry is my most potent trigger. One Sunday morning, while racing around the house like I was trying to win the Indianapolis 500 so we could get to church on time, my oldest daughter said to me, "Mom! We're just kids!"

Sometimes I expect my children to put their things away as quickly as I can, come upstairs as fast as I would, change their clothes in the same time I change mine. But the truth is, kid-time is slower than parent-time. And we ought to cut them some slack.

In an age when everything is instant—from communication and meals to ordering anything you want with a single click, no one is used to waiting—including me. Waiting has become a lost art. And teaching this to our children is most effective when they see it first in us.

In their book, *365 Ways to Raise Confident Kids*, Sheila Ellison and Barbara Barnett describe patience as "a deep breath that slows us down long enough to act wisely."

One breath can slow us down, redirect us and open the door for wisdom to walk in.

A Christian writer and mother of six, tells herself,

"I will not have any emergencies today. Life is not an emergency. There are no emergencies. Only amateurs hurry." - Ann Voskamp

I repeat this mantra often.

Several weeks ago the girls had no school. We had no lessons, no playgroups, no appointments, and I made the decision—no errands. We would stay home. We would put everything off that wasn't necessary and just be. In the early morning, I cracked doors to see if anyone was stirring. Curls fell softly around faces, small bodies burrowed under blankets, and I watched as they slept. I climbed onto the couch with a book and let them sleep until they wandered into the living room clutching blankets and smiling bashful. I hugged each girl then gathered the boys out of their cribs and we nestled onto the couch to read until we were hungry.

We made pancakes, poured the syrup thick, and sat together at the table, laughing. I wasn't lacing little shoes in between spoonfuls of cereal. I was present. Fully. And it felt so good.

We made plans for the day to stay in our pajamas for a while, do puzzles, play games, and then bundle into winter clothes so we could build something out of the snow in our backyard.

I held the boys longer than usual when putting them down for naps. I whispered in their ears, sang songs, and breathed in their baby scent—aware of their lengthening bodies and the way Spencer tenderly draped his arm around my neck. I washed dishes and watched out the window as the girls packed and rolled snow. They came in and out hunting for various accessories as three small snowmen took shape. When they finally came in to stay, we made hot chocolate.

The day was unusually peaceful, and I felt happy. The sun warmed my back as we built towers out of blocks in the living room. I saw things I am usually too hurried to notice, like the conversation my girls had when Sami gave up her favorite chair for her sister, the way Eliza told Ali her painting was "lovely," and the swiftness with which all of them moved to comfort a brother who fell, or needed a pacifier.

Instead of pleading "just a minute," I took Gordy's hand when he said "Mama!" and let him lead me to his pile of Legos so we could play. I laughed at Spencer's animal sounds and the way he giggled when Gordon poked his belly.

Sami joined me that night in the boys' bedroom. She sang them her own lullaby, and each girl kissed their baby brothers goodnight.

As I loaded dinner plates into the dishwasher, Ali perched on the kitchen table per her usual place and called my name.

"Mom?"

"Yes?" I turned to face her.

"I love you," she said.

An unusual sentiment for her and it split me wide open.

When will I stop racing through life? There is too much here. Too much to feel . . . see . . . listen to . . . and love. Life is made of moments. And there will never be another now.

I know we can't always amble through life. Down-time is not the norm. The typical day requires sticking to a schedule, a routine, and it's a challenge to get everyone where they need to be on time. But we can pace ourselves. We don't have to do everything the neighbors' kids are doing. We don't have to rush. We can decide on the right balance for our family and ourselves. We can quit looking sideways and look within.

Look Before You Lose It

While I was getting out of the shower one morning, the bathroom door opened, and my five-year-old poked her head inside to ask for a cookie sheet. "A cookie sheet?" I asked.

"Yeah . . . don't look mom . . . but we're making cookies for you. It's a surprise!"

My kids are usually asleep this time of morning, but not today. My girls were sitting atop the kitchen table making peanut butter cookies. Flour, peanut butter, and water were mashed into a glass bowl. The rolling pin was in full use, clumps of flour sprinkled the kitchen floor, and all three of my girls looked like little cotton balls for the flour on their pajamas and faces. Eliza had to be ready for school in a half hour and I now had an enormous mess to clean up.

Before I could say a word, the explanations came spilling out. "This was what we were whispering about yesterday Mom! This is our surprise! We wanted to get up in the middle of the night to make them, but . . . (tilting her head with a little question mark on her face), we didn't wake up!" Thank goodness, I thought.

I had been working on this tactic—the ability to look before losing it. So I gathered them around and thanked them for wanting to make cookies. I told them it was a sweet idea, but right now we needed to clean up the mess and get ready for school. I would help them make cookies another day, with all the right ingredients.

How could I be perturbed considering their intent?

As I vacuumed the kitchen floor, Eliza said to me, "Mom. I'm sorry. We probably should have asked you, huh?" She figured it out herself. No feelings were hurt, all relationships remained intact, and we moved on.

In every first-aid or CPR class, the first thing responders are taught to do is "survey the scene to make sure it is safe."

Checking the scene gives us time to examine what has really gone on, to ask questions, and determine intent. It helps us better understand the offender and the offended. We don't want to jump in too quickly and create another victim. We want to offer aid when the scene (and we) are safe enough to intervene. It also helps us see what is happening in our children's heads and hearts.

A few months ago, I set a consequence for my girls that exceeded the crime. I was hanging onto the day by my fingernails and as a last ditch effort, took away some privileges that hit hard. The punishment was more severe than it needed to be, and when Eliza was finally allowed out of time-out (privileges still not restored), she drew a picture for me that we now have posted in our kitchen. It's a crayon drawing of a bright red heart with blue background. In black letters she wrote at the bottom, "Feel the Love."

She was soliciting me for mercy, empathy, and love.

Looking before we lose it will help us discipline more fairly, laugh more easily, and, as taught to me by a five-year-old, "feel the love."

Set the Tone

Some days I fear the kitchen window will be open and my neighbors will hear "the real me" yelling at my kids. I don't think it's possible to always keep our wits about us and never raise our voices. But I do think it's worth trying.

I've noticed a pattern. When I raise my voice, my anger actually heightens. I get more worked up, and sometimes without warrant. A physiological response is set in motion.

Dr. David Hamilton, a clinical psychologist at the Christian Counseling Center of West Michigan says, "I suspect that if we hooked up equipment to measure our physiological response [when we yell], we would see a response similar to what we have when someone else yells at us."

He continues, "Yes, we can motivate people by yelling at them. (How else would we explain the existence of Little League?) It does motivate people to do something, but it may not be their best. It may motivate them to hide. It may motivate them to do what it takes to get us to stop yelling. If our goal is to help cultivate a lasting and positive change in someone, we don't want to start with showing them that we are out of control ourselves. Remember that no matter what the words are that come out, the message of yelling is, 'Please, someone calm me down because I can't calm myself down.'"

Learning to manage our voice is a matter of self-discipline. One mother I know describes anger as "lazy parenting." And I believe she's right. There is a better way. When I use a calm voice (it doesn't have to be sweet, it can be stern), the rest of me follows, and I act more rationally. Patience actually seems to breed patience.

Recently, my oldest berated her sisters because they didn't want to put on a "parade" with her. It was time to get ready for bed, her little sisters were preoccupied with books, and she was distraught over their disinterest. Her yelling probably merited a time-out, but I thought I would try something different. Instead, I asked her to come with me. "You'll feel better if you come with me," I said.

We went downstairs to her bedroom, and I helped her change into her pajamas, all the while talking gently with her about choices and "going with the flow" (a new phrase I tried to explain to her). I told her the parade idea was an excellent one, but she couldn't make her sisters join her. She could invite, but if they said no, she had to respect their decision. Maybe she could put her idea on the shelf for the night and try again tomorrow. We talked side by side on her bed, my arm around her shoulder, until her sisters came down to see what was happening. She hopped off the bed and said, "Guys. I learned my lesson. Would you like to do the parade another day?" They said yes.

Words matter. How we speak determines the tone of our home. Our children are made up of what we say and patience slows us down long enough to not only act wisely, but speak wisely—to be gentle with their hearts.

"The moment I am most repelled by a child's behavior, is my sign that I need to draw closest to that child." - Ann Voskamp

I am learning in life that those who need our love most, usually deserve it the least.

Dig Deep

I always wanted to be a mother. We struggled for many years to have children, and when they finally came, for some reason, God sent them all at once. But I am starting to see the wisdom in it—the beauty of all these children smooshed together. They are close, they have playmates, and they are learning to share and to wait. They are going to be better for it.

And so am I. Having five children in four years has been the hardest thing I've done. Nothing equals the exhaustion I've felt. Nothing has tried my patience and pushed me to the limit like being in charge of five very needy little people. But over time, I can see the snail-like progression of my soul.

On the most difficult days, I try to find those reserves that will help me do something or be something I think I can't. Kimberly Peterson, a Power of Moms writer describes it as "advanced parenting skills, a calmness that takes effect like a back up generator when the power goes out."

Mark Elliot Sacks said, "When everyone around you says you can't. When everything you know says you can't. When everything within you says you can't. Dig deeper within yourself and you find that you can."

The human spirit is remarkable.

Patience is like a well of power inside us. Each time we choose to accept what's been given, to slow down, to say no to something that will overextend us, to live in the mess, to lower our voices, or to laugh when we want to cry, the water in our well rises. When we give into the stress of the moment and lose our cool, we find ourselves parched, empty, and drained. Small victories add up over time, filling the well, rather than spilling its contents.

Last night I stood in the doorway of our living room and watched the thrum of our house—the hum of living that comes with five children. The kitchen sink was full of dishes. Goldfish crackers were crumbled into the carpet. Puzzles, books and building blocks scattered the floor, but my girls were dancing—wild and free—a flurry of limbs and laughter. A favorite song tripped a happy rhythm from the stereo, and I mused as both boys kicked and snapped their legs in an attempt to hoist themselves onto the coffee table. When they finally stood triumphant, they looked toward me at the same second and smiled, just to make sure I was watching. I clapped, blew them a kiss, and then leaned long against the doorframe.

Moments. That's all we have.

And I let the peace of this one warm me straight through.

＊ ＊ ＊ ＊ ＊

Feeding the Ducks

When I was a young mother with three children under the age of two, we lived in a one-bedroom apartment. I had just cleaned the apartment when I walked out of the bathroom to find Cheerios strewn all over my newly vacuumed carpet.

My two-year-old boy looked up at me, then deliberately reached his tiny hand into the Cheerios box, and proceeded to fling handfuls of Cheerios across the floor.

I lost it. I started ranting and raving about having just cleaned and how they weren't supposed to throw food onto the floor. I sat all three on chairs (they all seemed to be guilty), then spanked their bottoms for good measure. I must have let off steam for a good four minutes with them staring at me in amazement and confusion before I finally yelled, "Why? Why would you do this?"

Garrett, my two-year-old, answered, "I is feeding de ducks."

I proceeded to yell about that comment for another two minutes until I came to my next question. "Why? We don't even have any ducks!" Whereupon Garrett replied calmly, "They is ducks." I looked over to where my two little girls sat waiting patiently. Cali pulled her thumb out of her mouth and echoed Garrett's sentiments. "Uh-huh. I a duck and she a duck!"

Suddenly I could see how silly I looked to them. There was a logical explanation as to why they did what they did (in their minds at least), and I acted before asking them why. I've since learned to ask what's happening before I proceed with my disciplining. Sometimes it gives me enough pause to calm down that extra bit so I teach instead of yell.

- Sharla Olsen

Looking Back

I wish there were a way to take the wisdom of tomorrow and put it into action today.

Recently, my daughter and I were watching a video from a couple years ago when she was two years old. As we watched, I was struck by how beautiful she was—and how uptight I seemed to be! I listened as she pronounced all her words in precious two-year-old speech. I marveled at how much she had grown in just two years. She was so perfect then and so perfect now.

In the video, I saw this innocent little being trying so hard to learn and be part of the world. But as I listened to my voice, I heard a woman way too worried about small, insignificant things that two years later seemed to barely matter. I heard myself asking her not to make so much noise and correcting her for asking for something too forcefully. I heard a mother trying too hard, and saw a daughter beautiful, just as she was—noise and all!

"Why did that bother me?" I wondered. It was certainly no big deal—just some banging on the counter from excitement over the new toys Santa brought. She was slightly impatient with how long it took for my husband to pry her brand new doll out of the Fort Knox box it was tied in. When I saw how long it took my husband to finally free the toy from the packaging, I actually marveled at how patient she had been during the process. I was getting a little impatient myself just watching it! What was I expecting . . . perfection?

To only be able to go back and soak up that moment again! I would hug her, kiss her, and thank her for being so patient.

- Stephanie McKinnon

Lesson from the Left-hand Turn Lane

As we sat at the traffic light, waiting to turn left, a blind man and his dog taught me something I'd been trying to verbalize for some time.

A black seeing-eye dog, with his head down and ears alert, cautiously led this sweet man across a busy intersection. Everything stopped—all eyes, ironically, on them. I was touched that for a few moments everyone sat there, patiently, waiting for this man and his best friend to cross safely to the other side. Our light happened to be green, but no one moved. I was transfixed by this loyal companionship. I even got a little choked up as I tried to explain to my preschool aged sons what was happening. I wanted them to recognize the simple beauty of what had just happened.

My explanation was interrupted by someone honking. After a split second of annoyance with the impatient driver behind me, I realized that she must not be able to see what I could see. Once the man was safely across, the lady behind me sped up, and after catching my eye, waved her hand, smiled, and apologized. I waved and smiled back.

How many times do I "honk" at my children, having no idea what's in front of them? No clue what obstacle they might be facing, what hurt they are trying to mend, or what amazing spectacle they might be seeing in the grass at their feet? How many times do I honk my way through a busy morning, getting children fed, dressed, and off to our daily activities?

Has it ever hit you, like it hit me today, sitting there in the left hand turn lane? This whole thing, being a mom, isn't about me teaching my children. They're here to teach me. Every bit of patience I show is a measure of love that will be etched in their hearts forever. They may not remember the exact incident, but they will remember the color of my love – a soft, safe color that I hope is painted in their memories forever.

- Natalie Ellis

Connections

He shrugs a bit and twists slightly as I reach my arm around his shoulders. He is slightly taller than last week—his feet and arms growing faster than his torso, his thirteen-year-old body gangly. Still, I claim my goodnight hug and a kiss on the cheek before tucking the little ones in bed with storybooks and silly songs. In the morning, it's a short prayer together and my hand brushing across his forehead as he flies out the door.

And these moments, these brief touches, hardly seem to matter until the afternoon I'm stuck downtown and worry fills the phone lines as he asks, "Where are you? You're supposed to be home after school." Or the morning I sleep in and he tiptoes into my room balancing carefully on the edge of my bed to pray with me before he leaves for the school. Or those evenings when I notice him standing quietly in the shadows at bedtime, watching with a slight smile while Mary screams with laughter and Gabriel demands "one thousand kisses."

"You can scarcely imagine what it's like, mom," my nineteen-year-old son tells me, "to be thirteen and feel your body crackling with hormones. I couldn't tell who I was from one day to the next." But I do remember. I remember thirteen—an embrace, even from my parents, felt awkward as I grew uneasily into my body. I remember snapping at my mother and wondering why I was so impatient with my sister. That same look fills my younger son's eyes when he spits out cruel words and a moment later, recovers, shakes off the mood and seems confused at his unbidden anger.

With little ones, even the most outrageous temper tantrum is quickly followed by an opportunity to reconnect—dinner, a tub, clean towels wrapped around a tense little body, and stories and kisses at bedtime. Most parents innately recognize that children can't fully control their emotions and extend increased love after a necessary scolding.

Yet teenagers, whose bodies and emotions are as much out of their control as a two-year-old, are rarely offered the same compassion. By necessity, I nurture my little ones, but my teenagers, who I've carefully taught to pack their own lunches and wash their own laundry, can become quickly estranged if I don't make constant efforts to remain close.

And so, I unabashedly demand my hugs and kisses, the arm around the shoulder, the whispered prayer for their safety before school. Mood swings and fits of anger will come and go (or not) but my love for my children reaches deep, stretches wide, and like a mighty tree, offers protection through every storm.

- Michelle Lehnardt

PURPOSE

Chantelle Adams is a wife, a mother to four amazing children, an author, a youth motivational speaker, and a philanthropist. Ever since she was a little girl, she has wanted to make a difference in the world, and raising strong, responsible, compassionate children is helping her achieve that dream.

Giving back in simple ways draws her family close and provides countless moments of joy. Currently, she and her children have raised enough money to build a school in Africa and have started on their second school in Nicaragua with Free the Children.

Her passion is teaching kids, parents, and educators about leading by example, making a difference, and living a life based on key values. Her company, Foundations For Success Leadership Training (www.foundationsforsuccesstraining.com) has given her the perfect outlet to share this passion with the world. Her desire to make a difference also led her to become involved with The Power of Moms as the Director of Family Volunteering.

Chantelle believes that being a mom is the most challenging, yet most rewarding, work any woman can do. She says, "We are shaping lives and our future with every interaction."

CHAPTER FOUR

CELEBRATE YOUR UNIQUENESS
The Power of Individuality

by Chantelle Adams

"It is never too late to be what you might have been."
– George Eliot

A dear friend looked tenderly at old snapshots of loved ones—her late spouse, her children, her grandchildren, and her great grandchildren. She paused for a long time when she got to a photo of a young girl, about age three, with lopsided pigtails, crouching in a flowerbed with fistfuls of dirt. The little girl's smile was radiant, and her eyes twinkled with excitement and curiosity. The woman's eyes filled with longing as she looked at this photo of herself as a little girl. She looked up and spoke almost in a hush, "You see, I knew who my husband was, who my children and grandchildren are—and even my great grandchildren; but I think I lost track of who I was along the way."

Have we forgotten pieces of who we are? When we're so busy helping those around us become who they need to be, do we find the time to think about who we are and who we need to be? Do we know who the woman inside the mother really is?

"He who trims himself to suit everyone will soon whittle himself away."
– Raymond Hull

I think most moms have times when they feel sort of "whittled away." If we ever have a minute to think about who we are and who we want to be, we may find ourselves feeling a little lost and question who we've become and what more we can and should be.

But motherhood doesn't have to be about losing ourselves. It can be about finding ourselves in amazing ways. Our roles and responsibilities add to our character, and all our experiences assist us in growth and development. We are often taken down roads we never would have explored if it weren't for the responsibilities we undertake. The greatest of these responsibilities is motherhood—and it can offer us amazing opportunities to find ourselves and hone our skills.

The goal is not to simply *go* through motherhood. The goal is to *GROW* through motherhood. Following are several principles that I've found to be crucial in cultivating the Power of Individuality as we strengthen our own unique characters and talents as mothers.

Know Who You Are

"Our deepest fear is not that we are inadequate. Our deepest fear is that we are powerful beyond measure. It is our light, not our darkness, that most frightens us. We ask ourselves, WHO AM I to be brilliant, gorgeous, talented, fabulous? Actually, WHO ARE YOU NOT TO BE?" - Marianne Williamson

To embrace the Power of Individuality, we need to learn to define ourselves not just by what we do, but by who we are deep inside. Who have we always been, who are we now, and who are we meant to become?

We all want our children to have confidence and a strong sense of self, to be happy and rise to their full potential. Perhaps the greatest way for our children to understand and develop their own worth is to see our examples of being true to who we are.

One night, our family made little treasure chests. On yellow circles of paper representing gold coins, we each wrote our talents and abilities. We shared our observations with each other about what made each of us unique. The kids were busy writing when my seven-year-old looked up with a big smile and showed me what he had written. On top of his treasure chest, he had neatly printed the words, "Be Your Self." He knew the greatest thing about him was that he was an individual, and he was confident enough to just be himself. Don't we all need to realize this more fully?

If we are feeling lost or unsure of who we are, it can really help if we find some time to reflect and write some things out. With understanding comes power to renew our purpose and/or make changes.

One mom suggested this little exercise to help us find our true selves.

> *Try taking a few minutes to make a list of a bunch of the different facets of who you are. You could write it in your journal. What matters most to you? What do you love? What does your heart wish for? My list looks something like this:*
>
> - *I love to sing and play music.*
> - *I appreciate the beauty of nature.*
> - *I love getting outside; doing things like hiking, camping and walking.*
> - *I love to read.*
> - *I always try my best to answer when my kids ask "why?"*
> - *I want to live in a smaller home and spend extra money on traveling with my family.*
> - *I want to see more opportunities to serve and help my kids see them also.*
> - *I want my kitchen to be a gathering place in our home.*

Now think about how each of these things is—or isn't—incorporated into your life. Make note of what you wish was more evident. It might take time, but as you really ponder these things, you will start to see firm ideas rise up, distinct goals, and direct paths. You will feel the strength that comes from embracing who you are. You will feel the freedom of letting go of trying to be like other mothers around you. You will see much more clearly how, more than anything else, you are the right mother for your children and your unique interests and talents can benefit your family greatly.

- Terri-Ann Gawthroupe

As we take time to be still and really think about who we are and who we are striving to become, we will find confidence and an ability to intertwine our needs and desires with the demands of everyday life.

Accept that There's No One Right Way

Most moms want a lot of the same things for themselves, their children and their families. But even those who share our goals may have different methods that will get them to the same end. We're all different, and that's OK. It's a beautiful thing to celebrate other moms and their individuality and encourage and support each with love and admiration. I have gained a lot of wisdom and insight from watching and talking to other moms. Life is a process of discovery and as we learn from others and stay true to what resonates in our souls, we will find ourselves content and joyful.

The following story illustrates this point very well:

What possessed three busy mothers to channel their inner Martha Stewart, I'll never know. There we were with ten young children between us in a steamy kitchen—boxes of fragrant peaches daring us to process them. I guess we had visions of connecting to previous generations through doing what our grandmothers had done—plus, homemade bottled peaches sounded so good. Having gathered the necessary supplies, we entered the kitchen, confident that our efforts would be richly rewarded.

Of course, when we unpacked the glass jars, we soon realized each of us had some pretty different ideas about how to get to the shared end goal. Was it best to wash and dry by hand, boil and oven-dry, or use the dishwasher to sterilize the bottles? Should we remove the peel by individually blanching or dumping them in a sink full of boiling water? Halve, quarter, or slice? Light or heavy syrup?

After some polite discussion, we each decided to prepare our own batch the way we had been taught since we were each convinced our way was the best recipe for success. Hours later we emerged, sweaty, sticky and immensely satisfied with the fruits of our labors glistening on the counter in the late afternoon sun. Was it worth it? One bite left no room for doubt.

More impressive than the peaches was the principle I internalized that day: there is no one right way to prepare and preserve peaches! There are guidelines and basic principles that need to be followed, but allowances can and should be made for individual adaptation. And what's "perfect" in a bottled peach to one person might not be quite right to someone else.

Most mothers I know are all well-intentioned, talented women who want the best for their children and have their own unique ideas and methods. There is no ultimate, foolproof way to mother. There are however, plenty of good reasons to give ourselves, and others, room to personalize the parenting process.

In the end, we will all find joy in the fruits of our labors and the sweetness of our love shared with those who matter most. Although we may choose different paths and have different strengths, we can all get the same outcome of happiness and peace. We must pick the methods that work best for us and learn not to care whether or not others choose to do things the same way.

- Rebecca Owen

Define what Success is to You

Success means different things to different people. What is true success? Is it happiness, contentment, a peaceful home, a child who is confident, a family who makes a difference? What is your definition of success?

"Success means doing the best we can with what we have. Success is the doing, not the getting; in the trying, not the triumph. Success is a personal standard, reaching for the highest that is in us, becoming all that we can be." – Zig Ziglar

One mom shares a personal experience that teaches us to strive to achieve our own kind of success and our own personal best.

As a mother, you might think that "PB" stands for a sticky something you frequently spread on your child's sandwich. PB also stands for "personal best."

After having my third daughter, I was excited to get back into a regular exercise routine. I began a running/walking schedule and got to the point where I could run for 30 minutes nonstop, which was a huge breakthrough for me. But, I realized I needed a fitness goal: something to accomplish.

I always claimed I was NOT marathon material. They ran fast, I ran slow. They ran to win, I ran to recover. Running was therapeutic for me, so why would I want to run in a race where everyone was trying to run faster than me?

However, with my husband's support and encouragement, I realized I could run a half marathon as a fun goal and at my own pace. This is when I started to grasp the concept of "your own personal best."

Too often when I had tried to run with those "real" runners, I would come home feeling breathless and exasperated. When I realized I could run at my own pace and enjoy the scenery, I came home feeling happy and content. Interestingly enough, as I trained, my speed did increase, and I achieved a new personal best.

How often as mothers do we try to run at someone else's pace?

Sometimes we feel like we're not great "motherhood material" because we can't win the race. But how do we even define "winning"? Maybe we think we win the race by having the best-dressed children or the ones who always clean up their toys. Maybe we think the race is won by having teenagers who never question our decisions. But maybe we're striving to win someone else's race when we really should be figuring out how to win our own race.

Your own personal best is what you make it to be. Mother and nurture at your own pace and in your own way. If I start to feel that I can't keep up with what everyone else is doing, I separate myself and focus on what I am doing.

Then, when I feel I've achieved my personal best as a mother for the day, I feel happy and content…just as I did on those runs when I focused on running at my own pace.

In this fast-paced world, we can all use a reminder to find our own stride, to enjoy the scenery and to determine what constitutes our own personal best.

- Andrea Davis

Figure Out Your Individual Mothering Strengths

"To be nobody but yourself in a world which is doing its best, night and day, to make you everybody else means to fight the hardest battle which any human being can fight; and never stop fighting." - E.E. Cummings

Most moms I know, including me, seem to have a couple of tendencies that can stop us from benefiting from the Power of Individuality: guilt and what I call, "compare-itis". When we allow these tendencies into our daily lives, we get pulled down with feelings of inadequacy and discouragement.

When we compare, we often see others at their best and ourselves at our worst. We are trying so hard to do all the right things and be everything to everyone. In trying to be the perfect mother, wife, daughter, friend and woman, we often lose track of what really works for us and end up just plain stressed out. The reality is that there's no one kind of "perfect." We all need to strive for our own version of perfection—while cutting ourselves plenty of slack.

At a recent preschool activity, my son and I were sitting at a table with several little girls, age three, who were printing their full names using upper and lower case letters. My three-year-old son was as proud as punch that he could make a letter "T" which sometimes looks like an upper case and other times like a lower case, just depending on his connection with the paper as he rushes on to the next activity. I started to feel guilty that I hadn't already taught him to print his whole name and worried that I should have been spending more time teaching *my* three-year-old like these other kids' mothers must have done.

Feeling quite discouraged, I called my mom, which I often do when I am feeling like I don't measure up. My mom was quick to point out the good things my husband and I are doing. We spend time playing outdoors, going for walks, or riding bikes. We read with our children. We go on many adventures: skiing, boating, snowshoeing, motor-biking, and camping. We make sure to do service projects together as a family and talk about the needs in the world around us.

Then in all of her wisdom she said, "Remember to water the flowers, not the weeds."

How true!

I needed to stop focusing on what I wasn't doing, and focus on the things I *was* doing. I am doing my best in the best way I know how, and it works for my family. And you know what? I am letting my children embrace their individuality, too. Tanner may not be writing his full name yet, but at age two, he was riding his two-wheeler, skiing, and kicking a soccer ball farther than most kids twice his age. His individuality needs to be celebrated and honored just as mine does.

This mom shares some great insight:

> *There he was—my baby. So little, perfect, and helpless. The weight of what I was undertaking fell on me like a ton of bricks. It was so important to me that I do this—the most important job in both our lives—perfectly.*
>
> *The nagging little voice in the back of my head started with criticism and discouragement: "What were you thinking, quitting your job—the only thing you're actually good at—for diapers and housework? You're not a good homemaker, and you're no good with kids. You're going to screw him up, or scar him for life. . . ."*

Instead of banishing this voice, I listened to her. After all, she had some good points. I went into my journey of motherhood with one thought in mind: I won't be enough to raise my son the way he should be raised.

My early experiences with motherhood were sprinkled with some joy, but that negative voice came back time after time, because I didn't banish her. The first couple of years with my son were pretty rocky. I kept piling guilt and disappointment with myself on a growing heap of emotional baggage.

I didn't realize how destructive my negative thoughts were until after I was diagnosed with depression a few months before my son's second birthday. I actually believed it might be better if someone else raised my son.

Things changed dramatically for me when I came across the book "Mother Styles" by Janet Penley. She uses personality profiling to help mothers recognize their own way of mothering and how each style has its own strengths.

This book helped me realize that I needed to get to know myself better. I learned to recognize what aspects of my personality and abilities were real strengths in motherhood. I remember the tears flowing as I read this book, simply because the author used the word "strengths" when she was talking about my personality type.

As I read through the book, I found myself in those pages. I'm extroverted, so I don't like to be cooped up at home with someone who can't talk with me. I'm prone to focusing on thoughts, not feelings, which is probably why I find it difficult to relate to little ones who are so driven by emotion. I recognize the importance of a clean home and washing, feeding and clothing my kids, but as someone who likes the accomplishment of checking it off the to-

do list, I'm easily frustrated because these things are never "done" and end up on my list day after day.

I realized that the berating voice I was listening to was wrong: I'm not a woman who has no business trying to be a mother, and I'm not alone. I can be a wonderful mother in my own individual way.

This motherhood journey is a long one, and you'll exhaust yourself if you're trying to be something you're not. Penley said, "Discovering how to be a good mother based on your own nature instead of trying to fit yourself into some mold of what a good mother should be is the only viable approach for the long haul."

We should also keep in mind the term "journey." We can't expect to be great at something when we start out. Just like developing skills in other areas, like playing the violin or cooking, you have to practice—maybe a lot. Some things come more easily to certain people when it comes to motherhood. There are things I don't have a natural talent for—but if I assess these things and decide they are truly important to me and to my family, I can keep working on the things that matter and increase my abilities. That's the beauty of this motherhood journey; nothing will stretch you or help you grow more than motherhood because it is so demanding. And nothing else will do so much to help you become the best person you can be.

Motherhood is a big job, but perfection is not on the list of motherhood job requirements. You are the best thing for your family. Just keep trying, and someday you'll see the masterpieces you helped create—and the masterpiece you have become.

- Meg Talbot

We are each the perfect mom for our children. We certainly have things we can work on. But the individual talents, abilities, and ideas we each have are the raw materials we should build from as we become the mother and woman we really want to be—and the mother and woman our families really want.

I remember at the end of a very difficult day, I apologized to my oldest son for all the mistakes I had made. That sweet little boy looked at me with a puzzled look and simply said, "You are the best mom ever, I think you are perfect." My jaw dropped and tears came to my eyes. He could see that I was not only OK; I was everything he needed in a mom!

We are not perfect, but we are doing our best, and our best—not someone else's best—is exactly what our family needs.

> When we are able to embrace our individual mothering style and appreciate the uniqueness that is ours, we will find contentment and purpose in our lives. If we all mothered the same way, the world would be a boring place. I may not be contributing to society in the same way as another mother. I may not be mothering the same way as the mother down the street or across the world, but I am mothering in my own unique way, in my small corner of the world. And I'm OK with that. It's right for me. It's what I do.
>
> - Tiffany Sowby

Celebrate the Amazing Things Only You Can Do

"Enjoy the little things, for one day you may look back and realize they were the big things." - Robert Brault

I have always loved to perform, and when I am on stage in front of an audience, I am completely immersed in that moment. I live and breathe the feelings and emotions; I follow my heart and do what feels right. These moments on stage are part of who I am, but the majority of life happens off-stage, behind the scenes. I often catch myself wanting to hurry this stage of life, looking forward to the next stage instead of just enjoying the moment for what it offers. How often do we follow our heart or really immerse ourselves in our daily lives? I remind myself often to take time to really be present, to find joy in the little things that make life big, and to celebrate each moment for the gift it truly is.

One mom shares wonderful insight on celebrating motherhood and our individuality:

In Elizabeth Gilbert's speech, "Nurturing Creativity," she brings to life a wonderful lesson from the deserts of Africa. She tells of African dancers that would perform so magnificently that they would seem to transcend this very earth and appear almost God-like to their audience as they performed with such beauty and majesty. When a dancer reached what seemed to be the pinnacle of perfection in their performance, members of the audience would stand, clap, and shout, "Allah! Allah! Allah!" meaning "God! God! God!"

When the Moors invaded Southern Spain, this was a tradition they took with them. Over the centuries, the pronunciation was changed and the word "Allah" now sounds like "Ole'! Ole'! Ole'!" It continues today for bullfighters or flamenco dancers who give such splendid performances they seem to defy all human ability. "Ole'!" the crowd shouts and the audience knows it's a glimpse of the divine.

Then what happens? The next day arrives. The performance has ended. For the performer, the magic is elusive and hard to remember. There are the sore knees, the self-doubt. She wonders, "Will I ever ascend to that height again?" How could it be that just the night before she was lit from within?

Gilbert's take was this: There is a tremendous pressure from thinking you must ascend to such great height day after day. How can one possibly measure up? You can't. But what you can do is show up and do your part the best way you know how.

Gilbert's speech comes to mind often, dances through my subconscious when I'm feeling pressure to "perform." I am not an accomplished African dancer or bullfighter. I am a mother, a performer, if you will, on a different stage. How many times have I worked my magic at bedtime or while reading a story or while settling a fight? Haven't we all had those moments when we think for a moment, "Wow, I handled that beautifully!" Sure, that's happened. But how often has anyone witnessed it, clapped their hands, and yelled, "Ole'!" Hmmm. Come to think of it—never!

Neither praised nor witnessed by the world, my magic happens nonetheless, in those moments of motherhood. For these are the gifts I was given. And when we see those moments, we should recognize them. We should shout it from the rooftops—"Ole!"

- Amy Makechnie

Mothers don't get a whole lot of everyday praise or accolades. Only other mothers really understand the hard work we do and the hurdles we have to jump each day as we help our children and ourselves progress in often-intangible ways. We won't always get it right, but we can remember and celebrate the times that we do.

All of us experience little moments now and again when we catch a glimpse of the divine in ourselves as we use our own unique skills, knowledge and insight to help create amazing moments for ourselves and our families. We need to celebrate those moments and give ourselves a pat on the back when we see those beautiful little successes that make all the hard stuff of motherhood worthwhile.

Nurture Your Individuality—as PART of What You Do as a Mother

There was a point after having my third child where I found myself questioning who I really was. All my life I have loved performing, achieving, and doing. I come from an amazing family who are always quick to encourage and support me in my endeavors. I married a wonderful man, and we lived in one of the most beautiful places in the world. I had three remarkable children, and yet I found myself feeling the lowest I'd ever felt in my life.

I had just decided that with three children, I needed to stop doing all the other things that kept me so busy. I knew how important being a mom was and wanted to devote my full attention to this great calling. At the time, I was accompanying a choir, taking a writing course, dancing, organizing book clubs, group date nights and mommy groups, speaking, and writing a book—all on top of the duties of wife and mother of two toddlers and a newborn. It made perfect sense to say "no" to a whole lot of these things so that I could more fully say "yes" to motherhood.

But when I stopped all of these "me" activities and focused solely on being a mother, I felt lost. I was still plenty busy, but I didn't know who I was anymore. After really searching and seeking to uncover why I was feeling this way, I discovered that I rust out more quickly than I burn out. I needed to be doing things that were important to me while maintaining a balance with being a mother.

I can do the things I love, and I know why I am doing them; it isn't for the recognition or outward reward, but for the inward satisfaction of doing something I love and making a difference. I can find and develop my own talents while being the best mother I can be. Realizing that I needed to work on myself and still be true to me was the key in finding more happiness in motherhood.

This is a delicate balance and one that continually needs to be reviewed as our needs and the needs of our family are constantly changing. We all have different needs and bandwidths, and the amount of "extracurricular" activities that work well for one mom may be totally wrong for another mother. As stated before, comparing is a bad idea. But figuring out what types of personal-development and larger-world-focused activities we need in our individual lives is an important, great idea.

Here are some thoughts to help you figure out how to balance your personal development and contributions beyond your family with all that motherhood requires of you:

1. Write a list of all your dreams, goals, desires and ambitions. Then list them in order of priority, taking into consideration the season of life you are in and the realistic demands on your time. Choose the things that matter most and will fulfill you.

2. Get your family on board. Discuss with them how important it is for a mother to take care of herself so she can give her family her best. A wonderful example of this just happened this morning. I have a few deadlines pressing on me and was feeling a bit out of balance for the moment, and it was reflecting in my lack of patience getting the kids out the door for school. As I was raising my voice to a higher decibel and speaking with a less than desirable tone, my youngest looked up at me and in such a sweet voice said, "Mommy, do you need to go for a quick walk?" I burst into laughter and replied, "That is exactly what mommy needs, thank you for thinking of me." They understand that for me to be the best mother I can be, I need to take care of myself physically, emotionally and spiritually.

3. Make a plan. The best intentions will not help things to actually happen. You need to make a plan and set up the

necessary ways to make it happen. Maybe you'll need to hire a babysitter once a week or make sure dad can take the kids for an hour or two while you have a quiet space in your home or alternate with another mom to give each other time to learn and grow.

4. Find ways to weave your individual interests and personal pursuits into your family and daily life.

I appreciate this mom's understanding that we don't have to be gone or away from family to develop our talents and abilities, but we can find ways to do what we love while including our loved ones too!

While I had one small child at home, it was possible to find time during naps or late at night to pursue my own intellectual interests and hobbies. However, as my family got larger, I saw the amount of time left over for my own interests get smaller. I worried a part of me would need to be put on a shelf in order to accomplish the desire of my heart: to be a good mother.

Dr. James D. MacArthur said, "Teaching almost anything will eventually pay off, because the family sits down together and has a joint learning experience." This was a revelation to me and opened up a world of possibilities. If the teaching itself was the important part, then I could teach my children the things I knew and cared about. And even better, I no longer had to wait until my children were asleep to pursue my hobbies and interests. I could adapt them so I was teaching these things to my kids. I could be my own kind of mom.

I began to see that motherhood and self-expression didn't need to be two separate things. Thankfully, you can express yourself right in the middle of your motherhood.

Think for a moment about what makes you happy. What would you do if you had a whole day to yourself? Make a list of things you would like to know more about or that make you excited. What are you naturally good at? Now consider if some of these things can be adapted to fit within your workday as a mother.

If you love great literature, tell your children the story of the book you're reading, read classic children's literature to them, and write poetry and stories together. If you went to law school, maybe you could hold a family court or debate and talk to your children about the legal aspects of current events. If it is dancing you love, put a CD player in the kitchen and dance while you make dinner or make up a dance move that is unique to you and your kids. If you love art, take your children to museums, find great books about art that are kid-friendly, and create a "gallery" somewhere in your home to showcase the family's art projects—yours as well as the children's. Are you a foodie? Teach your kids about spices and cooking techniques and have a night each week when you cook with each of them individually. Nearly everything you love can be creatively adapted to include your children.

I saw my relationships with my children deepen as I introduced them to the real me. Also, I noticed my kids began to discover their own unique interests. They assumed if I was free to pursue the things I was passionate about, they were also. And they were right. Perhaps most importantly of all, I found myself growing and becoming a better person and mother.

- Heather Hosac

When we are true to who we are, that authenticity and passion will increase our ability to teach, love and encourage our children to be their best selves. Our example will shine through.

Just as we all have different answers to what means a lot to us, what we should pursue, what we're good at and who we really are, we all need to follow our own unique paths as we figure everything out. The principles in this chapter are quite universal and can help us find ourselves and celebrate ourselves in unique ways.

We can be who we are. We can do things our way. We can give our families and the world around us the greatest gift we can offer—the gift of ourselves—the *real* woman inside the mom—the woman that they really want and need.

Let us commit to finding ourselves, being our own personal best, prioritizing the pursuit of our own talents and interests, and cherishing our individuality. We'll be happier, better people *and* mothers as we do these things.

Hopefully, one day we can look back at our lives with a smile and know that cherished pieces of who we have become developed through the sum of our experiences—especially those of motherhood.

Mother, online communications consultant, social media obsessive, and entrepreneur, Chrysula Winegar is passionate about mothers and their capacity to change the world through simply raising their voices in families, communities, work, and politics. She blogs as frequently as she can, including writing regularly for the Huffington Post and the United Nations Foundation. Chrysula also champions global development issues for mothers and children at her mother activism blog, When You Wake Up A Mother (http://whenyouwakeupamother.com).

She truly believes that when you wake up a mother, you wake up the world. Chrysula and her husband have four children. She is Australian by birth and has lived in five countries and ten cities. For the last 12 years, she's been based in New York City and surrounds. Her husband says if she ever loses her accent, the marriage is over!

CHAPTER FIVE

AWAKE, ALIVE, AND PRESENT
The Power of Intention

by Chrysula Winegar

"Intention creates a mooring for our mothering. Moorings sink deeply into the ground and anchor a building or a ship in place. In the good times, or in the difficult times when we are in survival mode, our intents are holding us steady on course. They form the bedrock of our day-to-day living. Intent serves as a blueprint, a plan; an ever-present compass that guides us. Our intents are our deepest hopes for our children. And when mothers become clear in their intentions for their mothering, child rearing, and family culture, these intentions permeate our being and steer choices and actions. They fuel purposeful living and meaningful mothering."

- Elise Hansen and Abbie Vianes

An Integrated Life

I seek an integrated life. I define this as living and understanding my values; in other words, conscious, deliberate, proactive living. This goal requires me to understand who I am; what and who I value; what my purpose is in life. It asks me to live with intention, to anchor my behaviors on the shore of my best and most noble dreams.

I have four small children. Until recently, I hadn't slept through the night for eight years. I run a small business. I volunteer with my church and the kids' schools. I manage a busy household. I work with my husband in running another business. Sounds familiar, yes? There are days when my behavior is reactive, frazzled, angry and anchored in nothing more than exhaustion. Those are the days when my sense of vision is limited to how I *wish* things would play out, rather than the deeper purpose of what it is I am trying to create!

Of course, those are the same days when it becomes the most critical to breathe and stop and meditate on my greater purpose; on the mission I have chosen and recognized as my life's work.

There are moments when being a mother is the last thing I feel like being, even though I wanted this all my life, even though I love my children more than air. There are other moments when I am moved with such gratitude that these souls have been entrusted to me. And I remember. I remember that I chose this; that being a mother was a conscious, even fought-for act. I remember that being a mother is the most powerful role in society—a fact that society works very hard at concealing from us.

> *"Life is not about a position, it is about a purpose."*
>
> *- Cory Booker, Mayor of Newark, NJ*

I worked in a traditional corporate environment when I had my first two children. I loved the company I worked for, the people I worked with, and mostly enjoyed my work. I was very good at it, too. As my husband was setting up a new business, I was also the primary bread-winner for our family. As our second daughter drew towards her six-month mark, I was simultaneously reaching the next stage of my career. Two opportunities were presented: one involving extensive overseas travel; the other my dream job—but in another city—a move that would essentially scuttle our new business. It was crunch time.

I racked my brain through the possibilities and options, creating endless spreadsheets reflecting every scenario. My husband and I would make list after list of pros and cons. Deep in my heart, there was an enormous part of my soul that was pining to stay home with my children and to structure a career that gave me flexibility to mother the way I knew I wanted to mother, and work the way I wanted to work. There were many voices and harsh realities to consider.

What do You Want in Your Core?

My husband and I counseled with each other and consulted trusted advisers. Ultimately he challenged me: "What do you want in your core? What is the life we are trying to create here?" I knew the answer. Many years before, during another time of deep soul searching, before marriage, before children, I had spoken out loud to myself who I really am. An extract of my personal mission statement reads:

"I am integrated in thoughts, words and actions, especially as an example to my children. I partner with my husband to create a marriage that is organic but enduring, exciting but a sanctuary, eternal but daily progressing. Our children look to me with trust and honor, as a teacher and one in whom they find wisdom and safety. I teach them correct principles and facilitate their own abilities to choose the right."

The words I had written all those years before spoke deeply to me, and reminded me what I wanted in my *core*. That vision did not involve extensive overseas travel or a move to another city at that particular time. A seemingly impossible decision became instantly clear and straightforward.

I remembered who I was and my life's purpose. Not someone else's identity, not someone else's purpose, but the purpose I had already established for myself. I now work full-time again and love what I do; I just do it my way—a way that is highly flexible and honors my mothering.

Mothers with Purpose Are Powerful

Do you believe that? Do you feel it? Do you know what happens when a mother really embraces that truth? She changes generational patterns. She changes families. She changes men. She changes schools, communities, and churches. She changes politics. She changes countries. She changes the world. One heart and mind at a time. How does she do that? By acting on her life, rather than her life acting on her.

"We are mothers – women who sustain and lift and nurture. We are powerful, mighty in spirit, willing to risk all in order to raise up a generation of children who can overcome the challenges and trials of life." - Jenny Proctor

Do you recall those long months (years) of not sleeping when your children were infants? Perhaps you are just beginning this phase. There are those nights—we've all had them—when your child has cried for hours at a time, when you've been rocking and shushing and singing and patting. You're at your wit's end. And the next day, it doesn't matter how long you were up with your child in the night. His and the other children's needs must be met. Some basic home management and meals are required. There is work, a big meeting, important community commitments.

"Living deliberately means that we need to acknowledge that we are in a mothering phase of life. That doesn't mean that we can't or shouldn't do anything else. However, we don't want to wish our mothering years away." - Mary Christensen

In the midst of this period, we must realize we have a choice. We have power. We can't choose everything that happens to us, but we *can* choose our reactions and our approaches. We can dig deep into our reserves, into the vision we have for our family, and we can make mindful choices based on intimate self-knowledge of our values and purpose.

I don't know about you, but I don't always have the presence of mind in my exhaustion to make mindful choices. By evening of the following day, I can be cranky and grumpy and capable of a tantrum that would make any three-year-old proud!

But when I can keep my wits about me, I strive to simply figure out what's the most important thing I can accomplish—*what one thing matters the most right then*. I cling and focus on that one thing. How many times have you thought over and over in the midst of a crisis, "I can't do this, I can't do this" only to wake up the next morning or regroup at the end of a hard day having "done it"? Somehow you found the strength and maybe even noticed a little beauty along the way.

When we need to regroup, start over and find our flow, purpose is everything. Indeed, it is the only thing.

> *Do you ever make "to do" lists? I love making lists. They help me feel organized. They help me recognize what I've accomplished. They make me feel better about my day. Like mine, I imagine your to-do list is full of household chores and other obligatory responsibilities. Mop the floors. Go to the bank. Return library books. It probably also contains other things that aren't essential, but would still be nice to accomplish just the same. Finish book for book club. Run three miles. Work on baby quilt. Perhaps we also list a few things we would like to do for others. Bake bread for neighbor that just had a baby. Call the Aunt that just had surgery. Send a card to the Grandmother that just had a birthday.*

Would we mother differently if we applied the same sense of purpose to our children? What if our to-do list read: Listen to Henry say his ABCs. Ask Lucy about how things are going with that girl at school who's been giving her a hard time. Ask little John what he wants to do and go with whatever he's interested in for a few minutes. Look in Jordan's eyes and make sure he's feeling okay about his grades. Give five hugs. Say five positive things to each child. The list could (and should) go on and on.

From personal experience, I know that it is possible to be with my children all day, and then look back and realize I didn't actually spend any time with them. I didn't look in their eyes. I didn't really see them. To be present in body is not the same as being present in mind and heart.

- Jenny Proctor

What purposeful family-oriented things should be on your to-do list? If you don't thoughtfully consider the life you are creating, how can you know what it looks like?

"I made a list of the messages I want my children to remember from their childhood and home life when they are grown—the positive family messages they received as children, such as: 'I was always loved unconditionally,' 'my home was warm and inviting,' I could always depend on my mother.'" - Elise Hansen

What would you put on your list of messages you want your children to remember? How are they going to get these messages?

Mothering with intention has the power to change the mundane, the dreary, and the details, into stunning small and simple moments. It has the power to make the endless array of choices you face in the course of a day, clear and simple, stripped back to their essence.

Intent is like a stream that flows underneath the surface, unseen, yet flowing into our daily actions and choices. Busy mothers don't think about their mothering intents every day, but the power in this principle is still operating. There are times when all mothers, even those who have their intent firmly in place, feel like they are doing a terrible job at mothering—so what's the use? And their goal that day is to just get through the day without harming their offspring! So much for the loftier ideals of mothering!

This is exactly why spending some time as a mother, thinking about your intentions for your children, is crucial. Somehow the power of your purpose kicks in and is still working even on the days when all seems lost!

- Elise Hansen and Abbie Vianes

I focus on the people. I don't love the constancy of the messes. I don't like cleaning my house. But I love the people that make those messes. For them, I push through the drudgery. Each dish removed from the dishwasher is a dish that was used by someone I love. Each load of laundry folded and put away, a load of service given to those who I love. We must not blur the maintenance of a house with the maintenance of a family. If not checked, the tediousness of one can and will suck the joy clean out of the other.

- Jenny Proctor

The Tools of Intention

What does it take to create purposeful mothering? You will need to find what resonates for you. But here are a few tested methods that can help you craft your own vision and identify the actions and behaviors in your family that honor and support that intent.

Journal

If you already keep a diary or journal, then you have insight into the therapeutic power of a place to process thoughts, ideas, and dreams. It is not just the spot to record family events and cute kid moments (though that is important, too!), but it is a great tool to help you identify trends and themes that speak to you. As you write about your thoughts and feelings and process your life on paper, you will show yourself what it is you truly value. Through your own words, you will open up your mind to the possibilities of inspiration. Thoughts will drift in, when you are in that reflective space, that allow you to see who you really are.

On particularly tough days, that might not always be a rosy picture. But it's important to examine your negative thoughts. See what you can improve on, and throw the rest out. Guilt is a very useful tool in our lives—it shows us where we can do better. Guilt that moves us to action, that helps us change something, is a friend and gift. Guilt that weighs us downs, that paralyzes us and leaves us feeling hopeless, is useless and pointless. Let that kind of guilt go!

Note the joys, the moments to cherish and celebrate. Record feelings you have about the challenges in your life. Through this you will often feel inspiration and discover an idea or solution.

Mission or Vision Statement

A living, breathing declaration of who you are, both in reality and in aspiration, is a thing of beauty that you can create for yourself. Mission statements range from one sentence to paragraphs. Generally though, they are most powerful when stated in the present tense. "I am, I feel, I know" as opposed to "I will be."

"Have you ever made a list of goals or things you wanted in life, and you tucked it away in a drawer, only to come across the list some time later and be amazed at being able to check off some of the items? I wondered

how they got accomplished since I didn't proactively pursue them—yet it happened. That is the law of intent operating; it is an undercurrent that flows into our daily actions without necessarily being in our awareness."
- Elise Hansen

Living with vision infuses you with promise, with peace, with the reality of who you are now and who you can become. It is a place where the woman and mother you dream to be can take shape and form—and allows you to shift directions when life throws you the unexpected.

> *I grew up in a home with such an overarching value of independence and education; I had every intention of having my children well educated. I planned to teach them the languages I am fluent in and have them tri-lingual before they started school. We were going to hit it hard! And then I had two children with special needs who required intensive therapies and could barely converse in English!*
>
> *After the heartbreak and grief of lost dreams, I came to realize that their becoming multi-lingual was a goal stemming from my intent for them to be well educated. That intent is still in place but a course correction was necessary.*
>
> *- Elise Hansen*

Confidante

Bring your spouse on this journey with you. Our marriages are too often the last item on our lengthy to-do lists! In the desire to create intentional living for our families, and for ourselves, is a chance to envision a purposeful marriage.

It is never too late to start, and we must always remember that we are married to our husbands, not to our children. *The power of an intentional marriage can ripple through generations.*

Make time for your marriage. Schedule date nights and ensure there is time for intimacy. Being with your husband will often lead to those life-changing conversations only the two of you can have. As you talk about work, children, school, life, money, friends, and family, you are able to remind each other what it is you set out to do. And you remember you are in it together.

If you are a single mother, make sure you are still giving yourself a personal "date night" each week to renew your mind and soul. It can be as simple as a hot bath and some relaxation or some time with your journal. Invest some of your precious time in good self-care, your health, and education. Invite trusted friends and family into your life to share whatever elements of this journey that are appropriate to your life and to your mothering.

Your responsibilities are intense. There are always more tasks demanded of you than can possibly be managed. However, adequate rest and care of your body, mind, and spirit are utterly essential. The oxygen mask analogy is perhaps even greater in this scenario. Creating space to think and "be" helps you navigate away from reactivity, helps you mother with focus and power.

Inspiration and Meditation

Study the wisdom of great thinkers. Seek holy words that are relevant to your chosen faith. This does not mean bury your self in every self-help book or follow every guru. But inspirational texts and literature will lift your soul, open your mind, and plant ideas for the kind of woman, wife and mother you want to be.

Allow those words to enter your heart. Ruminate, reflect, and write about how they make you feel in your journal. Pray, mediate, and confer with the divine presence in your life—however that is manifest for you.

Do not walk this path alone. Allow the universe or God to be your partner. The answers will come. So often it is in this process that it becomes clear what a particular child needs right then and what your highest priorities need to be. Or how you should choose between a vast array of good, better, and best options.

These practices, in part and as a whole, strengthen you. They will help you discover and commit to your intention. They will give unlimited power to your life's work and help you adjust, change, and start over—again and again and again.

Time for Planning and Goal-Setting

"We need to take some personal time for ourselves as mothers and decide what direction we want our family to head. Perhaps it will be an hour once a week, maybe it is a weekend away, and maybe it is twenty minutes when you have locked yourself into the bathroom to think. We need to be deliberate in finding a time to plan our goals and direction for our families." - Mary Christensen

It's virtually impossible to run a business, a home, or a life in an effective, purposeful way if we do not take the time to process, re-assess, plan, schedule and set goals on a regular basis. The weekly goal-setting offered by The Power of Moms' Bloom Game is a fabulous self-assessment and planning tool. The Mind Organization for Moms program with its focused Weekly Review helps you move your projects forward and make your goals reality. Combined with a weekly planning and dream session with my husband, these elements help me keep moving towards my ultimate intentions and hold me accountable to myself.

Living and Breathing It: Holding on to the Big Picture

Does she really do all of this? Some days, yes. Some days, no! The mechanics of fitting it all in is different for each person. What matters is that each of these tools has saved my mind and my life!

I need to let go of wanting everything to be organized, to be perfect, and instead do some of the simple things that will make me happy. Sure a house of order is great, but life is passing me by while I pick up the toys for the 100th time or sweep the floor for the fourth time that day. I want to be remembered for living life, participating in life, and not for standing on the sidelines wishing I was out there doing it.

I knew having a large family would be a lot of work, and I would have to make sacrifices, but I really had no idea just how exhausted and emotionally spent I would feel some days. I rely on my passion for mothering to get me through. I think about what I believe in, what I hope to achieve, and what my dreams are for my family. It helps me to know where I should go as a mother, what changes I need to make, and what direction I should take in planning and preparing my children to be the best they can be.

As a mother, I find that if I stick to my passions, I feel secure, I feel at peace. I know what I need to do, where my time should be spent, and where I should go with leading and directing our family.

- Naomi Ellis

There is a plaque posted in our living room with our family goals. We all decided on them together. It reads, "Learn. Love. Laugh. Listen." It is something I cherish because each day as I look at it, I know where I am headed as a mother and what we are striving for as a family. It reminds me of what my intentions as a mother should be and gives me purpose in my life.

- Mary Christensen

The more we wrap ourselves in the tools of intention, and the more they become instinctive, the more patience we find—and the more joy we get to experience. In the moments of questioning what on earth we are doing and how can we possibly take another step, we can and should stop for a moment and ground ourselves in the sure knowledge that we are the right mothers for our children. *We are their mothers on purpose.*

The power of mothering and living with intention is having a vision for our lives and key relationships. It is refusing to live in a constant reactionary state. It is choosing to have control over our responses even when we cannot control the causes. It is making a mistake; as we do daily, even hourly; and regrouping, dusting off, and starting again. It is knowing who we are and lining up our doing and being with the glory of our possibilities.

* * * * *

Hot Yoga and Motherhood: An Intention for Your Mothering Practice

One evening, I was lying on my back and staring up at a high ceiling as a humid heat settled into every part of my body. The instructor walked slowly and peacefully into the room and welcomed us to our 60-minute hot yoga class. With a quiet, calm voice, she asked us to become aware of our bodies, to wiggle our toes and our fingers, and to become aware of our breath. She then invited us all to set an intention for the next 60 minutes of our practice. "It might be an intention of power and strength or peace and calm—but think of what your body needs right now from your practice and try to maintain that intention throughout." I absolutely loved the idea, and I now set an intention for every class I attend.

It is written in the Christian creation story that before every period of creation, God first set out his intention. God said, "Let there be light . . . And there was light." Bringing thought and intention before any type of creation, whether it be writing a poem, building a bridge, or raising a child, brings power and intelligence to your design.

I decided to try the principle out for the creation of my day with two boys, aged four and one. I sat down with a lovely little journal, a pen, and my awareness, wakefulness and presence. I looked at the blank page and thought about the blank canvas of a day that lay before me. I really thought deeply about what I wanted my day to be like. I thought about both what I needed from that day and what I thought my children needed from that day. The first thing I wrote down was the word Intention and then words I thought best described how I wanted to 'practice' my day.

One day, I woke up feeling tired and sluggish. I set my intention as slow but steady productivity, fresh air, create. Following my intention for the day, I ended up taking a leisurely walk with my kids to the local grocery store instead of driving. It was just what we needed.

I also wrote down the tasks I had to do that day: urgent and non-urgent. I wrote down the things I needed to pick up from the store and what we were having for supper. I wrote: let there be Lasagna . . . and there was Lasagna. I wrote: let there be clean laundry . . . and there was clean laundry. It felt wonderful to see on paper a plan and a direction to my day. On Tuesday my intention was activity and productivity. On Wednesday it was calm, joy, gratitude. On Sunday it was refresh, rest, connect.

Setting up a type of mission statement for my day has been not only helpful in giving structure and direction to my days, but gives me a space before the commencement of each day to connect with myself and the divine.

From this practice, I've felt direction and insight come to me as I invite my intuition to aid me in my efforts to understand my family's needs as well as my own.

- Charla Majeran

Your Own Wondrous Story

There is a quote that I love that says, in part, " . . . Your own wondrous story has already begun. Your 'once upon a time' is now." I am in the middle of my "happily ever after," and one of the most beautiful and anticipated parts of my wondrous story is in full swing.

I am a mother. I have two of the cutest, sweetest, most headstrong and obnoxious little girls of all time. They are 15 months apart, and most days I love their closeness, while other, less often days, I wonder what in the world my husband and I were dreaming the day we said, "Yeah! Let's get pregnant again right now!"

When the day begins, I have visions of getting up an hour early to get showered and dressed before waking my girls and getting them breakfast. After breakfast, I will whisk them upstairs to do their hair with adorable bows and flowers and then choose an outfit that matches those bows and flowers from their perfectly-organized closet, so we can head to the park to play.

Instead, I don't wake up until Olivia comes into my room and throws her sippy cup at my head yelling, "I need water!" I then shuffle in to get Lucy out of the crib and head downstairs for breakfast, hoping the blinds are closed because I forgot to put on any pants. After Olivia has used her yogurt as lotion and hair conditioner, I realize that I am supposed to be meeting my friends at the park in less than half an hour.

I pull Lucy out of her high chair and accidentally dump what seems like eight hundred mandarin oranges, which I thought she had eaten, onto the floor, which I'll have to clean up later. I tell Olivia to climb out of her high chair because, quite honestly, I don't want to touch her. We head to the bathroom, where I stand them in the tub and do a quick wipe down. I then put Olivia's hair in two ponytails with only one bow because I'm hoping I'll find the other one as I go through my make-up drawer. Lucy gets one ponytail so that I only have to find one bow for her.

I put on my make-up and blow my hair around, hoping it looks like an on-purpose messy, and head to find my pants. By this time, I have three minutes before we have to walk out the door, and I notice that Olivia has pulled both of her ponytails out. I put them back in, but can no longer find even the one bow, so she will be bowless today. I rush into the girls' room and paw through the mountain of laundry, that I have such good intentions of hanging up, to find a couple of pretty-close-to-matching outfits.

I dress Lucy, and in the process snag her hair and pull half of the pony-tail out. I'll fix that later. I find Olivia behind my dresser with some chocolate (I am completely baffled as to where she got it) and find that she has pulled her hair out again. I put her clothes on and rush with her and Lucy to the car.

We get to the park and start to unload. I realize that I only *thought* that I had shoes in the diaper bag, Olivia had more chocolate stashed that I didn't know about that she has smeared all over her face, and Lucy's ear is still covered in yogurt. As my barefoot, filthy, and scraggly-haired children and I walk over to meet my perfectly coiffed friends and their equally well-dressed children, I wonder how in the world they do it. They laugh when I ask, as though my question is such a silly thing. For them, beauty is effortless. This used to bother me. But I embrace it now. Because I know my purpose.

I could spend a lot of time at the park staring at the cute little bows that my friends told me they made just that morning to match the new outfit, but that wouldn't serve my purpose. There is a stark difference between desires and purpose. My desire that morning was to have everything go perfectly before going to play at the park. My purpose was to love my babies and spend time with them. And I accomplished that.

We all have different backgrounds, different talents, and different passions, but we share purpose. Often we set our expectations on what the ideal scenario should be to accomplish a certain task. Then, when our children decide to throw a tantrum, or refuse to tell us the chocolate stash hiding place, or don't cooperate in some other manner, we feel we have failed. We feel that we aren't doing things correctly or we aren't doing them as well as we think other mothers are doing them. But there are many different paths to happiness.

In our day-to-day lives, when the best-laid plans go awry, or things really aren't turning out as we thought they would, we can waste time waiting for things to get better, or we can pull ourselves up and go out and create our happily ever after . . . whatever it may be.

- Aubrey Glaus Sanfilippo

Then I Remembered . . . I Am the Mom

Sometimes I look around my apartment in confusion. Where am I? How did I get here? Usually this is around 8 am when we are transitioning from disaster and attempting to create order. We have been up for a couple of hours, and I wonder how we got to this point. The dishes are clean—but piled precariously on towels from last night's clean up. Piles of books and an empty milk sippy-cup are surrounded by a well-loved pink blanket placed in perfect tripping range right at the hall way entrance. The baby is soggy and kicking fiercely—grunts and squeaks to let me know she is still here. My husband is long gone—the only signs a damp toothbrush and a lingering scent of aftershave.

I can see my daily "to-do" list in the corner of my eye—it is so long it is threatening to teeter off the page, and I still have four things ticking in my brain. We have only one hour to be in the car and out for the day, but first we need to get three girls cute, start a load of wash, nurse, pack the diaper bag, be cheerful, and ignore the mounting piles of random "stuff" that mysteriously accumulates each day in my bedroom. I try to show patience—gritting my teeth as I tip toe around the scattering of clear marbles down the hallway, and yet still manage to land a hard poke in the arch of my foot.

I sometimes wonder why I am here, because I love order—and this is anything but organized! I thrive on being able to 'handle anything,' and yet find myself overwhelmed multiple times a day. I give a longing glance to my pillow, suck in a deep breath, tie up my disheveled hair in a ponytail, and face the day because I have to. Because I want to. Because I just remembered . . . I am the Mom. I am the mom. I am THE Mom.

It is during those cold sleepy early hours when I hear the baby, squeaking and grunting protests of an empty tummy. I roll over, drifting back into my dream because "that can't be for me. . . ." The next shriek from the bassinet jolts me to reality . . . that is my baby, and this is my life. Moments later, only half alert and sleepy, I am overwhelmed with the knowledge that yes, I am the Mom. My arms have found what they were looking for—as if holding this sleepy nursing baby is what they were made to do.

Sure there are days that I wonder what it would be like to go 24 hours without having some Disney song stuck in my head. It would be delightful to have a trip to the grocery store sans meltdown at the candy checkout. Finding time to workout any time of the day would be a dream, and church would definitely be much more enlightening if I got to actually hear the messages. Many nights I go to bed guilt-stricken and worried, convinced I have stunted my child for life because I did or didn't do_____.

Despite these hiccups and imperfections, I am still the Mom. One day I'll send them off to make their own choices and find their own ways. I know that I will miss these early days: the funny conversations, the creative play, the crazy energy and happy shouting, the baby cuddling and cozy story telling. The early morning bed-heads, first time giggles, and the outstretched arms requesting "Momma, you carry me?" These are the memories I want printed deep inside me; these are the parts I hope will never fade. Because I get to be The Mom.

- Danielle Porter

Purpose and Intention after Tragedy

My life has been drastically changed through the birth and death of our third child, who was born just shy of 25 weeks and lived a brief 30 minutes before passing away. My time spent with him challenged me to think about my purpose as a mother, my intentions with all of my children, and how I was going to move on from this tragedy.

It has forced me to not just mother, but mother with a purpose—to do good and be good. During this difficult time, it helped me realize that I still had other children I was responsible to nurture and raise. I knew that I needed to still move forward with life and be the mother for my other children. There were days I struggled, days I couldn't find the strength to be the best mom I could be.

Part of moving forward with a purpose means acknowledging those bad days, pressing onward, and vowing to have a better day tomorrow.

- Mary Christensen

To-Do List

Breakfast. Kids to school. Dishes. Laundry.

Change diapers. Vacuum. Sweep. Tidy up. Phone calls. Pay bills.

Run errands. More diapers. Kids home from school.

Help with homework. Dinner. Dishes. Bath time. Bedtime.

Busy. Busy. Always busy.

Mommy! Mom!

Stop. Listen.

Breakfast. Kids to school *(Looking for cloud pictures . . .)* Dishes.

Laundry *(Snuggling in the warm clothes)*.

Change diapers *(Tickles and giggles)*. Vacuum. Sweep *(Sing a song together)*. Tidy up.

Phone calls *(Let the machine get it—we're reading stories)*. Pay bills.

Run errands *(Help push the cart)*. More diapers *(This little piggy went to market)*.

Kids home from school *(Sit, share a snack)*.

Help with homework *(Mom, how do I . . .? Let's figure it out)*.

Dinner *(Please pass the . . . I had so much fun today . . .).*

Dishes. Bath time. Bedtime *(Lullabies and stories, hugs and kisses. I love you).*

Busy. Busy. Always busy.

Busy together.

- **Karen Stavast**

Shawna Woodworth was born and raised in Tucson, Arizona, the last of six children of a university professor and an elementary school teacher. She is now the mother of three children, ages seven, five, and two, with one more on the way. She and her husband, Jed, spent the first nine years of their marriage growing their family in Madison, Wisconsin, before recently transplanting to the Mountain West.

Shawna met Jed in Chicago, where she was teaching high school math and Spanish in an inner-city public school. As difficult as that experience was, she has found mothering to be the great challenge of her life. Writing for The Power of Moms has helped her to process experiences in a meaningful way, thereby developing her skills and understanding of motherhood.

Meanwhile, mothering also allows Shawna the flexibility to do a little bit of everything else. She has taught group aquatics exercises for the Arthritis Foundation, tutored high school math students, taught music at a Spanish-immersion preschool, and competed in several racquetball tournaments. Shawna loves to wow her kids with original cake art, talk domestic politics with her husband, and is an avid reader of the *New Yorker* and *The Week* magazines.

CHAPTER SIX

GROWTH HAPPENS NATURALLY
The Power of Progress

by Shawna Woodworth

A deep yearning for progress comes with being human. Our babies start out utterly helpless and then learn to roll over, crawl, walk, laugh and interact, all in the space of one year. Our children want so much to read and ride bikes and become "big." Ambition and accomplishment are part of human nature. Mothers feel this as much as anyone.

Far from wanting to merely "coast" through life, repeating mindless routines for twenty-plus years; moms feel deeply the urge to progress—to grow stronger, wiser, and deeper—as individuals and as mothers. We hold on to our individual dreams and abilities and merge them with our desires to progress through motherhood.

The progress we make as mothers and as individuals often seems imperceptible from day to day. And that makes sense. Our babies grow without anyone perceiving the countless changes happening inside them on any given day. Yet the *accumulation* of days reveals the dramatic outcome of all of those tiny changes!

The same is true for mothers. We can be certain we will progress through motherhood because all living beings grow, given time and the proper nutrients.

Here I'll focus first on the progress we make as mothers, and then talk about more proactive ways we can progress as individuals.

Part I: Our Progress as Mothers

What more important realm could we strive to progress in than motherhood? We want to improve as mothers because so many are counting on us. Our work will influence not only our children, but many of their friends, and even other parents, families, and societies going forward—no pressure!

Moreover, our own experience in mothering improves as our mothering abilities do. The more confident and able we feel as mothers, the better we will enjoy the role.

A Rough Start is Normal

I spent my youth idealizing motherhood as I watched my sisters and other hip moms work with their kids. I practiced what I saw them do and became a favorite baby-sitter to children of all ages. I could not imagine loving anything more than being a mom.

But my initial entry into motherhood was not what I expected. The baby-sitting and my subsequent training as a high school math teacher did nothing to soothe my crying baby or get him to sleep. There were no other parents to come home and relieve me of my baby-sitting duties (except my equally-baffled husband). And my college education and previous work experience were futile. My son didn't care that I could graph a quadratic equation three different ways!

Sure, I'd read plenty of parenting books, but I had zero *experience* caring for another human being so small and entirely dependent on me for everything. When my son was ten days old, I actually scheduled an extra doctor's appointment, just so that for those thirty minutes, my baby could be in the hands of someone who knew what she was doing! Those early days and months as a new mom were awkward and overwhelming.

As shocking as my initial feelings were, I can now reflectively say, they were normal. I know dozens of moms whose experiences were similar to mine.

Motherhood, like other professions, follows a growth-curve much like the chart at the pediatrician's office. Naturally, the most growth occurs at the outset. A new mom, like a new teacher or a new doctor, has to study and think carefully through every detail of her role that comes easily to seasoned mothers. Previous experience may help some new moms learn faster, but true competence and confidence requires many hours of on-the-job training.

The very concept of growth implies starting smaller and weaker than where we end, so it makes sense that we might feel inept at first. And with each additional child or "new beginning" in motherhood, I've found some of those feelings return. While the awkwardness does not feel comfortable *at all*, I have learned to endure and accept that those feelings won't last forever.

We CAN Be Taught!

One of the gnawing worries of my early mothering years was that I might just be a bad mom. I would look around at other moms who seemed to thoroughly understand and enjoy their mothering work, and think, "Uh-oh, I'm not that good."

What I didn't realize was that I was just a quality-mom-in-training – and that I will be training for the rest of my life! I had everything to learn, and motherhood had everything to teach me. When a woman becomes a mother, it's like she's enrolling in a special brand of higher learning—Mom University. Mothering surrounds her with unique opportunities to learn that she couldn't have any other way.

In her book, *Mindset,* psychologist Carol Dweck argues that we all have a choice to live with either a "growth" or a "fixed" mindset. By adopting a *growth* mindset, we can overcome limitations, develop essential talents and even see failure as an opportunity to learn something new. The promise that we *can* learn and progress offers hope to any discouraged mom. Here are just some of the ways that we learn through motherhood.

Learning through Reflection

Much of what we learn as mothers comes through personal epiphanies as we puzzle about our mothering challenges. Some of my best insights come to me when I just sit down to think—usually with a notebook in hand.

I've found that, deep down inside, I *am* tuned in to the deepest needs of my children, and it is in meeting those needs that I develop myself as a mother.

It was in a reflective moment recently that I realized my three-year-old daughter was being under-served by the regular neighborhood play-dates she clamored for. What she needed was a mommy who could focus on helping her to develop her mind. So instead of just sending her next door whenever she asked, which was my habit, we started a little "mommy" preschool, just the two of us. The curriculum was simple but focused: sing the ABCs, say one nursery rhyme, read two books. My daughter absolutely blossomed during that small daily exercise.

Nobody told me to do that, and it's not something I did with my other kids. I just sensed *she* needed it. Our time together in that setting has already become one of my most treasured mothering memories. We are closer, her mind is turned on to learning, and I developed skills as a mommy-teacher in the process.

Looking within and finding answers builds confidence in our ability to meet the challenges of motherhood.

Learning from Other Mothers

We can help each other to progress as moms. At Mom-U, all mothers are teachers, students, professors, and colleagues. Our first, most influential professor is often our own mother, and we learn from countless other examples as well. Mothers further along the experiential curve share their seasoned knowledge, and younger moms, their noses in the parenting books, also offer spot-on ideas.

We share "what works" at play-dates and soccer games, in book groups and learning circles. The Power of Moms website, as well as personal blogs, offer forums for sharing mothering insights. Often just considering how to report an experience to someone else leads to fruitful reflection.

Virtually every parenting challenge we experience has been experienced before. Parents everywhere have found solutions, even if they haven't written a book about them. As we find solutions to our own parenting challenges, we are positioned to share our insights with others.

As a "newer" mom, I always appreciate when other mothers teach me from their experience, as this mother does:

> When a five-year-old has chapped lips and her mother is fighting with her to stop licking them, I calmly say, "Let's try some of this fancy cherry Chapstick—it smells really good and it will make your lips feel smooth. Just don't lick it or it won't work anymore!" I now easily handle the same argument I had with my daughter when she was younger. A positive spin takes little effort and can make all the difference in the world.
>
> - Karin Schelling

Learning through Trial and Error

At Mom-U, we each have our own laboratory—our home—where we can test out various parenting theories and ideas. Starting from the parenting philosophies of our own parents, we explore other ideas in books or from moms at the park and test them on our kids.

Sometimes this experimentation is painful because we often make mistakes—even if we start out with a sound theory! But for the most part, if an experiment fails, we needn't worry that the laboratory will shut down. We can just log the failure as useful data and try something different the next time.

Jim Fay and Foster Cline, creators of *Love and Logic*, advocate allowing kids to learn through experiencing the "natural consequences" of their actions. As mothers, we get to do this too.

I will never forget the day I let my two-year-old son dump all the pieces to ten wooden puzzles at the public library. "He'll learn not to dump out puzzle pieces," I reasoned, using my best parenting-book understanding, "when he sees how hard it is to put them all back together." But of course, on that day, it was *mommy* who learned that toddlers are not capable of putting so many puzzles together by themselves. (Duh.) And after they quickly tire of the chore, it becomes all yours.

Lesson: When your baby starts to dump puzzles, INTERVENE!

The beauty of mothering is that we *can* learn from our mistakes and avoid them the next time. The very repetitive nature of mothering affords us multiple chances to improve and do better until we get it just right, kind of like Bill Murray's character in *Groundhog Day*.

Success teaches as much as failure. Once, while trying to get sluggish kids to pick up toys strewn about every end of our small apartment, I said on a whim, "Let's see how much you can get done in five minutes—I'll set the timer." Wham-O! Instant results. Only later when observing a more experienced mom use the same technique did I realize what a motivational gem I'd discovered. Her independent experience led to the same conclusions mine had.

Our daily practice as moms helps us create a mental catalog of strategies that either work or don't. Serendipitous strokes of inspiration add up, creating a pool of effective mothering techniques to draw from.

Learning through BEST Practice

As any musician or athlete can attest, the best way to acquire a new skill is to practice it. But merely "putting in hours" day after day doesn't lead to progress. We need *Best* Practice: personal *exertion* in which we actually perform the skills that we are trying to master, to the best of our ability.

We cannot hope to become even-tempered mothers, for example, if we never practice the discipline of holding ourselves together when we feel like exploding. Sure, there may be instances when we let loose and breathe fire, but there must also be times, hopefully an increasing number of times, when we *will* ourselves to be calm, at all costs.

It is when we succeed in performing well in the most difficult circumstances, and then string together a number of such successes, that we acquire real mothering strength. Aristotle said, "We are what we repeatedly do. Excellence is therefore not an act but a habit." And habits, at first, are formed one decision at a time.

Along those lines, I appreciate this mother's epiphany:

> *If I want to change results in my family, then I have to do something different. That may sound funny, but doing the same thing over and over and expecting things to be different*

> *does not produce the improvements I want in my family.*
> *- Penny Tapp*

We likely already know what changes we want to practice, though we face resistance at first because our children are often used to our old ways and respond accordingly. Persistence is really the key to developing any good habit, as was so famously stated by Ralph Waldo Emerson:

"That which we persist in doing becomes easier to do—not that the nature of the thing has changed, but that our power to do has increased."

The journalist Malcolm Gladwell found research to support Emerson's claim, suggesting that ten thousand hours is "the magic number for true expertise" (Gladwell 2008, 40). Citing examples of international phenoms, such as the Beatles and Bill Gates, Gladwell argues that the common denominator in their enormous success was approximately ten thousand hours of rigorous practice in their respective fields.

While our work may not receive worldwide acclaim, mothers have a similar opportunity to develop our own mothering genius. If we devote our time with children (which is certainly more than ten thousand hours!) to practicing our best parenting skills, we will develop into the mothers we hope to be.

Be Assured . . .

You've Come a Long Way, Baby!

Much of our progress as mothers will be discovered only in retrospect. We can see our own evolution when we look at a mental snapshot from a blog or journal page three months or three years ago.

Consider all the skills a mother of a newborn quickly masters, beginning with learning to wash that floppy, slippery little body. We learn how to nourish a baby, and how to help her rest; how to comfort her and express love with songs and coos.

Improvement comes with experience. We get better at one-sided conversations and playing the little baby games that elicit the sweetest giggles. We learn to do almost anything one-handed while baby rests on the other hip. We get faster at cleaning up nesting cups (and all the other baby accoutrements that seem to take over the house!), and we become more skilled at finding acceptable "trades" when baby has something she shouldn't.

Before long, mothering an infant begins to feel natural. And then our baby becomes a toddler, so we hit the books again! As we gain competence at each stage of parenting, we can remember those initial awkward feelings as a measure of growth.

Along with the skills directly involved in childcare, we also improve our skills as homemakers. We may never learn to *like* scrubbing floors or washing dishes, and that bottomless pile of laundry with all its mystery stains could defeat even the most determined chemist. Still, as time passes, we find new and better solutions for keeping up. We work on training and motivating our families, hire help, or just get better at doing it all ourselves.

Your Weaknesses Can Become Strengths

Perhaps like no other experience in life, mothering helps us grow strong in the places we are weak. For one thing, we have a new motivation to be our best selves: our children are depending on us *and imitating us!* Kids ingeniously unearth our weaknesses and bring them to the forefront.

My friends and I sometimes joke about how "patient" and "compassionate" we were before we had children. When those qualities were challenged, we realized we weren't nearly as polished as we'd thought! Mothering experiences lend themselves to gradual refinement and useful attributes that stand the test of life. A friend of mine put it this way:

What skills have I significantly improved over the years through mothering?

- ***Empathy:*** *I have sat in the middle of a sidewalk on a busy street holding my two-year-old motionless while she screamed and tried to hit, kick, bite and head butt me. It's a bit harder to judge other parents now that I have been there.*
- ***Mind reading:*** *It is a skill, really it is, and I can do it with my kids. Based on their behavior, I can tell if they are hungry, tired, cutting a tooth, worried, happy, need an extra story, want a piece of candy or have to go to the bathroom. I can tell if it is time to leave a play date, take away a toy or have some special mama time.*
- ***Civil political discourse*** *(or discourse of any kind): I do not want my daughter saying things like, "He has stupid ideas," so I don't say those things about political candidates with whom I disagree . . . even if they get elected. I talked to my daughter about saying things like, "Congratulations. That was an impressive win," and "I disagree," and "I think you are wrong," without shouting or adding little personal attacks. I am getting better at keeping my mouth shut until I figure out how to remain civil without belittling my strongly held opinions.*

Jesse Boyett Anderson

Probably any mom could create a similar list of advancements. An important item on my list is compassion. I have learned how to care for my kids when they're suffering, even when their pain is self-inflicted, and even when I could say, "I told you so." This brand of compassion did not come naturally to me at first, but practicing consoling words and comforting actions has made me more nurturing.

Mothers of children with special needs model in a unique way how experience makes a mother grow strong. Perhaps nobody expects their child to have special needs, and few feel prepared at first. But I have watched one friend after another rise to the challenge.

When my first son was born, a good friend of mine had a baby with Cerebral Palsy. Everything from feeding and resting to movement and exercise required special handling and medications. At first, I'm sure, it felt overwhelming, but I watched her quickly adapt. While caring for her son has required many sacrifices on her part, those very sacrifices and his place in her life have helped her to grow strong and focused as a mother.

Your Imperfections Make You Perfect

It is easy to underestimate the value of learning on-the-job. After all, I think, wouldn't my kids be better off if my Fairy Godmother would just wave her magic wand and make me a perfect mom? Wouldn't it be nice to just *be* a perfect mother instead of going through the grueling process of *becoming* one?

The truth is: imperfections perfectly qualify us to be life-coaches to our kids! We must help them deal with living in an imperfect world, surrounded by imperfect people, including *themselves.*

When they see us struggle to learn something or overcome our own mistakes and even failures, we teach them how to do that too. Our own bewilderment with motherhood allows us to empathize with our kids' struggles to figure out life.

As we work through the process of becoming better mothers, we become the models our children look to for learning how to manage missteps. We will grow and improve, and we can shower them with assurances that they'll acquire life skills too, one new understanding at a time.

Measure Your Progress Carefully

Sometimes the most difficult part about progressing as a mom is finding a way to measure our growth. How do we measure progress according to those things we can control, and not the things we can't?

Should we feel dejected about our mothering efforts if our family members don't shower us with praise? Can we measure our progress against the practices of the mother next door? Do our children have to perform academically, socially, religiously, athletically, musically, and so on, in order for us, as mothers, to feel a sense of accomplishment?

If we judge ourselves by looking at the behavior of others, we may resent family members for not living up to our expectations—or attempt to control their choices. We may try to find validation by pursuing other activities where success is more easily measured, and consequently limit our ability to serve our families. Or, we may decide that mothering is a wasted effort and simply give up.

Thankfully, there is no single, agreed-upon goal of parenting against which we "pass" or "fail." Our real progress as mothers is not measured by the actions of our children or our neighbors.

I learned this from a friend who describes her mothering experience in this way:

> *When we had our first child, and we started to feel confident with our parenting skills, we thought we could see what the "successful" outcome of our parenting effort would look like. We had our own dreams and aspirations for each child.*

But the years taught us that our kids get to choose their own path, and that path, for various reasons, may not match the path that we initially defined as our, or their, success. So we have to shift our paradigm. This process doesn't mean we have been negligent or unsuccessful parents—it just means we were a bit naïve and didn't fully understand our kids' individuality.

- Shelley Hoffmire

If our objective is to establish effective, loving relationships with each of our children, then we can work toward that no matter what kind of life choices they make. We may become more attuned to the needs and moods of individual family members and respond in more gentle ways.

We can gauge our progress according to how focused we are on each child's unique needs and how effectively we are mentoring them through their current challenges. We may find more pleasure in the seemingly thankless service we render to our children, even in everyday tasks.

We may not be praised for the work that we do, but our conscientious efforts will yield a more satisfying fruit: the peace of mind that we are doing all in our power to fulfill our roles as mothers. That is success indeed.

Part II: Our Progress as Individuals

OK, now I'll admit: it's really impossible to set our progress as mothers against our progress as individuals—they are so thoroughly intertwined. So much of what we do to develop ourselves as mothers helps us to become better rounded individuals, and vice versa.

In many ways, motherhood is *ideally* suited to personal development—contrary to popular belief.

For example, the moms I know who are actively pursuing a college degree report that they are more focused students because they are mothers and more focused mothers because they are students. They manage to squeeze more learning into shorter blocks of time because they must.

In her book, *The Mommy Brain*, journalist Katherine Ellison shows how pregnancy and early motherhood actually remap parts of a woman's brain by boosting our perception, efficiency, resilience, motivation and emotional intelligence. We become more capable leaders as we plot our family organization and manage the many competing claims to our time and attention.

So when I speak of progressing as individuals in this section, I'm really talking about the things we can do to be *proactive* about our progress as individuals and as mothers. Managing pursuits outside of our mothering realm won't happen without our determined effort. And while it's true that we will naturally get better at mothering, even those abilities can be systematically enhanced with concentrated effort.

Measuring progress in personal life can be difficult for anyone. Even mothers who have periodic evaluations and external benchmarks in another career are left to their own devices when it comes to measuring personal progress. Programs like the "Bloom" game on The Power of Moms website can help, but ultimately, personal styles will dictate how we go about it.

Lovers of grand plans might measure progress with charts and figures. Those who live in the moment may let feelings of contentment be the reward. Women who prefer to spend all their time doing the "mom thing" might focus on advancements there, while others might reserve set blocks of time for other ambitions.

However you approach personal fulfillment, here are some things to consider.

Think Big Picture

Sometimes we are strangers to our own deepest desires. It's easy to let the rush of living, and the near-constant demands of our children, quash our inner lives. By setting aside some time to focus on the larger view of our lives, we can discover how we truly want to invest our time.

Some people find a "vision" useful to guide in decision-making. A vision can take many different forms, but its purpose is to remind us at critical junctures what we most want in life. With a vision, we can measure our own progress against the potential that we see within ourselves. This can be mapped out in advance or created as we go along.

Here is how one mother made her vision tangible:

> *After visualizing different scenarios in my mind, I created a vision board with a collage of different things I wanted in life. My vision board hangs in my bedroom directly across from my bed so it is the first thing I see when I wake up, and the last thing I see when I drift off to dreamland. Just this morning I was looking at my vision board, and I noticed that there were at least ten different things I had accomplished without realizing it, all because of those positive, subliminal messages I had been sending to my brain every day.*
>
> *- Megan Stewart*

Creating a vision is like choosing a college major. Both provide a framework for moving toward larger goals and competencies. In life, as in college, sometimes people know their major from the start, while others figure it out after taking lots of classes. Still others change their major many, many times, as their experiences change them. These are all understandable scenarios. By affording ourselves time to think, our deepest desires will rise to the surface.

Establish Goals of Varying Shapes and Sizes

If creating a vision is like choosing a major, then setting goals is like creating a class schedule. Goals help us choose between competing goods. Accomplishing a goal can be the most easily-measured form of progress. Some moms like to set written formal goals; others just have a general sense of what they are trying to accomplish. Even a hastily-scribbled checklist can be validating at the end of a day's accomplishment.

I like the variety of potential triumphs on this mom's list:

> *I look for my own personal growth when I celebrate my little moments of achievement. Most of these moments are simple:*
>
> - *Cooking a new recipe*
> - *Making time for exercise*
> - *Finishing a book*
> - *Staying calm in difficult situations*
> - *Finishing a reasonable to-do list*
> - *Catching up on paperwork*
> - *Spending quality time with a child who needs it*
> - *Keeping up with the bills*
> - *Getting everyone to an event on time—or at all*
> - *Getting everyone home from an event!*
>
> *- Naomi Ellis*

And when you're ready to set some larger goals, perhaps focused on a vision you have for your life, you might try some of these ideas:

To help me set goals every year, I choose a one-word theme, such as Simplify, Choose, Embrace, etc. Then I consider several categories – physical, spiritual, mental, emotional, financial, interpersonal, etc.—and set some specific goals in each area in line with that year's theme.

I try to limit the number of big goals, and I cross them off as I either accomplish them or decide that a particular goal is no longer in line with my vision. I hang my goal board next to my bed (yes, my room is full of foam core décor) where I can refer to it often. It keeps me motivated and also helps me see what I've already accomplished.

Another fun and effective way to set goals is to break them up into years. What do I want to accomplish ten years from now? (Then five years, two years, one year, etc.) Recently I found some goals I had set five years ago. Everything in line with my vision had been accomplished.

The best part is your children watching you do this! This past summer, my boys wanted kittens from the neighbor so bad, they finally convinced me by deciding to do a goal chart to earn them. I have never seen a three-year-old quit sucking his thumb cold turkey like that! I was so proud to watch them stick to their goals and see them grow.

- Megan Stewart

One friend of mine sets goals motivated by subject area. She selects a topic she wants to learn more about and then applies her free time to mastering the subject. As soon as she feels she has sufficiently mastered one area, she chooses another subject to pursue. In ten years she has become well versed in finance, gardening, music teaching, food storage, swimming, small business, ethnic cuisine, racquetball, and more. She is never at a loss for new goals to pursue and her passion for learning is contagious.

Whenever I see a mom who is learning and doing so many impressive things, I am always tempted to just adopt all of her plans as my own. But I try to remember that I'll get more satisfaction out of meeting goals that match *my* talents, interests and circumstances. We can be inspired by other moms without pressuring ourselves to do all the same things they are.

Get Started

Starting a new goal can be the hardest part because it's easy to feel pulled back by our responsibilities at home or other circumstances—just when we're on the brink of doing something grand.

If you're not sure *where* to start, try this:

> ***Create a Bucket List***. *Write down everything you have ever dreamed of doing. The first bucket list I ever made included riding in a hot air balloon and seeing a Broadway production of* Les Miserables. *Within months of creating my list, both of those opportunities presented themselves through conversations where I mentioned my desire to do those things. Inspiration and opportunities that might have been previously overlooked are brought to our consciousness when we write things down.*

> ***Invite Others to Participate***. *When I decided to take guitar lessons, I discovered that my son's second grade teacher shared that goal. We were able to take lessons together, splitting the $80 per month tuition. Another time, some friends and I were discussing how we wanted more opportunities for our children to serve. After that conversation, one mom put together a day for us all to gather and bag lunches for the homeless. When we talk about our goals, we are likely to find others with the same dreams.*

Do SOMETHING Today*. We might be tempted to put off living our dreams until the time and circumstances are just right. While there is definitely a time for every season, you can still approach your goals by breaking off bite-sized pieces. For example, earning a college degree might not be a viable option right now, but perhaps you could interview professionals in the field, learn about local programs offered, or read a book on the subject.*

- Rebecca Kohler

I aspire to improve my mind and further my education, but registering for formal classes won't work for me right now. So I've tried to find ways to develop my mind on my own.

I've joined book and discussion groups with other moms, and I try to read as much as possible. A mom-friend and I try to stay conversant in current events by challenging each other to read news periodicals, with the promise to talk about what we read during our weekly conversations. I know other moms who read professional journals to keep current with other careers and listen to audio books (especially in mp3 format) when they're too busy to sit.

My favorite tool in personal development has been a three-subject spiral notebook. I use the first section to record academic or world-related learning. The second section holds spiritual insights gained from church or worshipful study. And the third section is devoted to professional development in mothering and homemaking. I take notes from parenting books, plan out schedules and routines for my family and record epiphanies there.

Whether I choose to study a single topic extensively or just read and think about whatever comes along, I make a record of the things that I'm learning so that years down the road, I can remember the learning acquired during these busy years!

Dare to Soar!

Once we lay out our vision, set some goals, and begin, we might be surprised where life takes us. Sometimes we only have to take a few steps before the really rewarding opportunities open up.

Any goal worth pursuing will involve some amount of sacrifice from self and family. We may find that our goal causes more strain than it's worth to us and decide to cut back (which is itself a worthwhile form of progress). On the other hand, we may find that our ambition takes on a life of its own and propels us toward success!

I love this mother's experience:

> *When I first dared to write a book, I had a new baby and two little boys. I wrote late at night and early in the morning. Eventually, I found a way to reproduce a few copies of the book myself. While picking up the newly-bound books at the copy shop, I bumped into the owner of a gift shop who invited me to do a book signing at her shop. So I started making lots of books! A local copy shop would print and cut them. I hand-made all the covers.*
>
> *At one point, my handmade book ended up in four different shops around town. I found myself doing more book signings and enjoyed radio and TV interviews. I then tried to find a publishing house to pick up the manuscript. While that didn't pan out, by doing that search, I was hired by one of the publishing houses to be their Literary Publicist.*
>
> *When we choose to dream and take the steps necessary to make the dream REAL, our lives change, and before we know it, we are no longer the person we used to be.*
>
> *- Wendy Christensen, Author of "It's the Little Moments that Matter"*

While some life goals may have to be postponed or even cast aside to make family life manageable, women can and do experience and achieve more than they might anticipate with kids in tow. Maybe we can't do *everything* we always dreamed of doing, but we can always do *something* to make those dreams real.

The Magic of Mother Nature

Our progress, like that of our babies, comes in fits and starts. There may be long stretches where we see no noticeable progress, but those will likely be balanced with periods of intense growth. As we develop the skills and habits that enrich our lives, we gradually become the person we have always wanted to be.

I'm only six years into this mothering life, so I think I'll have more to report about my own progress after a couple of decades. But so far, I am convinced that motherhood makes the *world* a better place, not only because of the nurturing we offer to the future adults of the world (our children), but because of the people *we* become in the process.

I love the classic image of that saintly grandmother—the woman with silvery gray hair pulled up in a bun. She is *so* wise, knowing the right answer to any question, seemingly able to accomplish any task. She knows how to respond to human suffering in any form, how to balance discipline with love. And how did she become that all-knowing grandmother?

By being a mother first.

ORDER

Jennifer Cummings loves being a mom to her beautiful daughter Anina. Their favorite pastimes include playing the piano, simulating cooking shows, making movies, and coming up with any activity more fun than cleaning.

Jennifer received a Ph.D. in communication and family relationships, with an emphasis on mother/daughter relationships (which comes in handy in her personal life!) from the University of Utah, where she has also taught for over a decade. She is a co-editor of the book, *Hope After Divorce,* and enjoys working as a communication consultant.

While being a single mom brings unique challenges, she is profoundly grateful for the close bond it also brings. She is grateful for the help of her parents and siblings, whose support makes it possible to be a little closer to the mom she wants to be. She feels especially blessed to have a mother whose wisdom and sense of humor continually help her to take seriously the things that matter most and learn to laugh at everything else.

Jennifer is inspired by her daughter's love, trust, goodness, hope, excitement, humor, resilience, faith, joy, and all-around adorableness, and cherishes the unique privilege of being her mom.

CHAPTER SEVEN

BALANCING THE BALANCING ACT

The Power of Balance

by Jennifer Cummings

I love the things that fill up my life. I love raising my daughter. I love being with my family and friends. I love my work. I love volunteering. I love walking. I love that the list of things I love is too long to name. A full life is definitely something to celebrate!

The struggle for me, and I think most moms, is when our full lives start to overflow.

As a mom, I have learned that there will always be more to do than time in which to do it. I really can't recall a day since childhood in which I truly felt caught up. Still, I hold out hope that by approaching my life with the right principles in place, I can keep up with the demands.

What I am seeking is *balance.*

Even the word evokes a reassuring sense of calm. Unglamorous as it sounds, while others dream of cruises and winning lotteries, I dream of stopping the clock long enough to empty my in-box, cross off every item on my to-do list, make dinner from scratch, read a book, and play with my daughter until she gets bored (which has never happened!). But time marches on whether any of that happens or not.

In truth though, if my life had to be perpetually organized and up-to-date before I could feel balance and contentment, I never would. Some degree of organization, structure, and predictability is obviously a necessity, but what I (and all of us) need is a strategy for achieving a sense of balance when life's pulls inevitably come from all different directions—often at once.

You Have to Name It To Claim It

Wanting a more balanced life is a noble goal, but an elusive one, until we decide what balance is and what it is not.

Balance is not simply the product of good time-management or organizing strategies. These are helpful tools in the process, but balance is more than just having an orderly life.

Balance cannot be imitated or faked, and pretending we have it does not benefit us. Balance cannot be given, and no amount of money can get it custom-made and delivered to our door.

Sometimes we feel our life is balanced if we are able to check off the majority of our to-do list. And while managing to cram it all in is no small accomplishment, this is usually not the kind of balance that satisfies our soul.

Ultimately, balance must be earned. And in my experience, re-earned again and again and again.

For me, balance is living an abundant life in thoughtful proportion. It means having relationships, responsibilities, interests, and goals, and striving to have the wisdom and discipline to put appropriate emphasis on, and boundaries around, each.

Above all, balance is a condition of the mind and heart and soul that comes from knowing what matters most in your life, then behaving in ways harmonious with that knowledge.

That said, my life is nowhere near as tranquil and coherent as my definition would suggest. In fact, the irony of me "preaching" about balance will not be lost on those who know me best. While there are times when the intersections of my life flow in and out of each other like a well-choreographed dance, there are also times they look more like a six-car-pile-up.

Granted, we all have a million things to do, but that's not the point. More important is the fact that we are constantly choosing between worthwhile things. I find myself toggling between extremes of all the things on my "list" and double-checking myself to see if I'm striking the right balance between it all. Maybe in your own quest, you've asked yourself these same questions:

"Do I work too much? Should I play more?"

"Am I too easy on my kids or am I too strict and need to lighten up?"

"Do I give enough to my community/church/children's school? Does my family need me more right now?"

"Should I use the time I was going to _____ (work, garden, repaint the study, read, return email) and instead _____ (make dinner for a sick friend's family, visit with my elderly neighbor, chaperone my child's field trip, research science fair possibilities, go to the Neighborhood Watch meeting, figure out how to use the new video camera)?"

The demon that haunts many a mom is not just whether we've done everything we need to do; it is whether we did the *right thing* at the *right time* and in *proper proportion* to the other things on our to-do list. That, for me, is the biggest challenge in finding meaningful balance.

Every few years I re-read Anne Morrow Lindbergh's classic book, *Gift from the Sea.* I love her observations about life as a woman in which she elegantly captures our yearning for balance:

137

With a new awareness, both painful and humorous, I begin to understand why the saints were rarely married women. I am convinced it has nothing inherently to do, as I once supposed, with chastity or children. It has to do primarily with distractions. The bearing, rearing, feeding, and educating of children; the running of a house with its thousand details; human relationships with their myriad pulls—woman's normal occupations in general run counter to creative life, or contemplative life, or saintly life. The problem is . . . basically: how to remain whole in the midst of the distractions of life; how to remain balanced, no matter what centrifugal forces tend to pull one off center; how to remain strong, no matter what shocks come in at the periphery and tend to crack the hub of the wheel.

What is the answer? There is no easy answer, no complete answer. I have only clues." (p. 29)

Like Lindbergh, the mystique of balance intrigues me, yet, I too have only clues. As she gained her wisdom from the sea, I have similarly found many of my "clues" from observing the physical world. Some help me achieve greater balance and some help me feel at peace when balance eludes me. My clues are not comprehensive, but I hope they may be helpful as you too seek for balance in motherhood.

Clue #1: Live By Your True North

Just as our earth rotates on an axis that is centered on the North Star, we can better balance all of our priorities by finding a central focus for our lives. Author Stephen R. Covey refers to this as finding "True North," or your center—that part of your life that you focus on foremost so that everything else can assume its proper place.

Our first challenge as mothers striving for balance is to determine what our True North axis will be. For me, living by my True North means living according to what I know to be right. It means making life decisions intentionally, not by default. Knowing my True North gives me the courage to focus my energy where I believe it should be, not according to what is popular or pleasing to others.

My True North is family and God first. When those two things are center-stage in my life, everything else falls into place around them—so even if the rest of my life is off kilter, I can at least feel balanced inside. As this mom puts it,

"Having internal balance does not require having balanced circumstances. Even amidst chaos, we can feel peace." - Lizzy Richards

Knowing our True North can ease the decision-making process because we have already prioritized who and what in our lives will win out when the pressure is on. Knowing my True North kept me on course while plugging my way through graduate school. As a divorced mother going back to school, I committed early on that I would put my daughter first before my schoolwork. I was grateful to get my education, but I determined it would not be at the expense of missing her childhood. This was not an easy balance to strike, with sleep and free time being two of the biggest casualties—but with my True North in place, I found success in school while being the mom I wanted to be to my daughter.

Even with my commitment in place, however, there were growing pains and moments when my sense of direction was compromised. One afternoon, my daughter, who was not always fond of naps but very much needed them, resisted sleep. I scheduled my homework during her naps, and on this afternoon I needed to get three chapters read. Sleep evaded her, so I resorted to driving her around in the car to put her to sleep. After a good hour or so of driving she finally dozed, and I drove home anxious to get going on my chapters. As if on cue, my daughter, who usually slept through the car-to-bed transfer, woke up. Without missing a beat, she was wide-awake and ready to play.

Looking back now, I shouldn't have cared so much about three silly chapters, but I did, and they hijacked my focus. In my frustration, I turned to my own mom to vent, saying something thoughtless about having wasted two hours trying to get my daughter to sleep—and all for nothing. My mom's reply penetrated me to my core. She said simply and gently, *"Time spent with your child is never a waste."*

I thought I had my True North in place before that day—and, in fact, I did—but what I realized then is that staying true to what matters is not a one-time decision. It is a daily commitment, renewed again and again with each choice.

Staying true to our True North is not always easy. For me, it meant getting through school slower than my peers, passing up tempting professional advancements, and foregoing certain luxuries, hobbies, and a social life. But it also meant having a closer relationship with my daughter and a clear conscience from not abandoning my principles and priorities. It even yielded better performance in school and work. Living true to what you believe is the only way to achieve real success at anything—and motherhood is no exception.

Clue #2: Say "YES" to the Season You're In

"To every thing there is a season, and a time to every purpose under the heaven" - Ecclesiastes 3:1

I like the idea that we live our lives in seasons. It is comforting to know there is a time and purpose to every phase of our lives. Of course this implies a good deal of patience on our part. Just as we can't enjoy autumn's vibrant colors in April, or picnic on a soft grassy lawn in January (at least where I live), neither can we expect to have all the treasures of a lifetime of seasons packed into today. Allowing life's opportunities to blossom in their proper season helps us appreciate the present. It allows us to focus on who we are, and whom we are with, right now. To be constantly wishing away the current season, because the next season seems more appealing, is to miss the fragrance of lilacs after a spring rain because you can't wait for barbeques by the pool.

As Linda Eyre wisely reminds, *"Life is long. You can have it all—but usually not all at once."*

I believe in this principle, but it can be harder in practice. Like many moms, I have a long list of hobbies I'd love to pursue and projects I'd like to complete. I'd love to learn to play the guitar, research my family history, learn another language, develop my career, volunteer more, travel, clean out the attic, garden, and play tennis every week. And of course, I want to do all the things on my list NOW.

Having everything at once is not a recipe for balance, though. Our lives fill to capacity quickly, and if we aren't careful, instead of us running our lives, our lives are soon running us.

When my daughter was very young, I didn't travel a lot, exercise regularly, or spend much time developing myself through education or work. Instead I held her for hours, took her on walks, read to her, spent long afternoons with family and friends, got my house in order, and kept a journal. Occasionally I longed for the "productivity" of earlier seasons, but mostly I relished the uniqueness of a season in which slowing down was necessary—and even encouraged.

Since then, I have experienced many seasons—each offering different opportunities than the last. My daughter is now in school, which means I have blocks of time to focus on endeavors like my own education and career, exercising regularly, and reconnecting with friends. This season is also busier than ever, as our daily routine has expanded to include homework, piano practicing, clubs, chores, and recitals. In fact, those hours sandwiched between school and bedtime often feel like an episode of "Minute to Win It!"

But I love the season I am in.

Helping my daughter learn a new song on the piano is exhilarating. Lying on her bed, talking about her day, her friends, and her dreams is priceless. Having a few hours to myself to work at my job or on a project is a luxury.

Eventually, we realize the fleeting pace at which seasons that once seemed endless pass like a dream. As this mom reminds, today's demands often become tomorrow's yearnings.

> *Crying babies and sleepless nights will only last a short season in our lives, and then it is us who will be longing for midnight snuggles. Battles with teenagers soon end, and we will long for those late night discussions. The home we once wished would just stay clean will soon feel all too empty.*
>
> *"Today is a gift; that is why it is called the present." – Unknown*
>
> *- Chantelle Adams*

Enjoying the bounty of the season we're in prepares us to receive tomorrow's blessings more fully because instead of looking backwards with regret at what we missed, we will be looking around with gratitude at what we have.

Clue #3: Prune the Garden

Pruning the garden is what makes saying "yes" to the season we are in possible because it means saying "no" (or at least "not now") to everything else.

I am no gardener, but the one gardening task I thoroughly enjoy is pruning rosebushes. I love taking a good pair of loppers to an overgrown, ill-shaped rosebush and transforming it into a trim and tidy version of its former self. One purpose for removing old branches from the rosebush is that they drain nutrients from healthier parts of the plant, making it harder for the plant to grow and reach its full potential. Careful pruning not only removes the unproductive limbs from the bush, but it can increase the number and quality of a plant's blooms. The effect in our lives is no different. When I begin to feel like I am doing a lot of things—but none of them well, I know it is time to prune. This means letting go of the things I really don't need to do now in order to cultivate something better.

Pruning my garden has meant parting ways with, or seriously limiting, non-fruit-bearing habits like TV and online social networking. Scrapbooks and overgrown file cabinets have also been temporarily set aside until today's work subsides. Pottery classes and extensive travel have been shelved until a future season. There is not enough time and energy to feed all of those branches now . . . but their time will come.

Too often, we let someone or something else decide where we ought to put our time and energy. One mom suggests the following ways to protect our time.

Before taking on new commitments, ask yourself these questions:

- *Does this really matter?*
- *Do I WANT to do this?*
- *Does this really need to be done by ME? Am I really the best person to do it?*
- *Does this really need to done NOW?*
- *What will I NOT do so that I can do this?*
- *Can I do this in a simpler way? Is it worth doing well or just barely worth doing?*

Once you've made an intentional decision about what you will take on, try to hold strong to the following:

- *Set boundaries around the things to which you have committed yourself. Share the boundaries with your family and ask them to help hold you to them*
- *Reserve time for doing things that "fill your well" as well as fulfilling your family's needs*
- *Watch out for the "It'll just be for a couple of weeks that I'll be working like this, then I'll take a break and really enjoy my kids" trap—that can stretch on and on*

And finally:

- *Protect time with your children—that is time that will never come back*
- *Replace the old saying, "Never put off 'til tomorrow that which you can do today" with a more fitting motto for mothers, "Always put off a put-off-able in favor of a now-or-never."*

- Saren Eyre Loosli

Motherhood is filled with now-or-nevers—irreplaceable firsts, fleeting lasts, and everything in-between. Perspective is everything in making sure we cut off anything that will sap precious energy from the thing that matters most today. Getting the sweetest, juiciest fruit is possible when our energy and focus are not drained by lingering, fruitless branches.

Clue #4: Find Your Rhythm

There is a rhythm to motherhood. Some moments call for an upbeat tempo, others are more like a march, and still others wind about at a soothing crawl. At times, we dictate the rhythm, and our families dance in step with the beat we set. Other times, our children's rhythm out-sings our own, and we fall in line with the beat of their drum. Being in tune with the rhythm of your family and your rhythm as a mother is essential to finding balance.

One of motherhood's greatest dilemmas is how to balance being "productive" with being "connected"—two different rhythms indeed. In more practical terms, we wonder . . . should I get my work done (housework, paid work, paying the bills, etc.) or drop everything and play with my children? Both are important. Both are necessary. At times, work trumps everything else because bills are due, deadlines loom, or there are no clean clothes to be found. Other times, play trumps all, and we drop everything to play hopscotch or checkers or just talk.

Unless you hire it all out, most of us can't get by without "doing" the mom stuff—it comes with the territory. Fortunately, to a reasonable extent, many of us like this part. I (mostly) enjoy doing the physical labors that make my daughter's life easier, richer, and happier. I find a lot of satisfaction in accomplishing chores, completing projects, checking off to-do lists, and just plain serving my family. Furthermore, much of our emotional connection with others comes through *doing* things with them, for them, and around them.

Still, there are times when your family doesn't really care if the laundry is done, if dinner is simple or elaborate, and if Mom is caught up on her work—they just need Mom, the listener, the cheerleader, the counselor, the playmate, the companion. They need her focused and undistracted—as if she exists solely for them in that moment. This is as much the work and joy of motherhood as is raising soccer stars, musicians, and children who know how to do their own laundry, write a thank you note, and balance a checkbook.

Consider this formula for knowing when to "do" and when to "be."

Multi-tasking is a mother's best friend. Anytime I can get two things done at once is pretty exciting. I fill potential "wasted" time with something I enjoy, like reading a book or magazine while I wait in the parking lot to pick up my kids from school. When my children arrive, I feel refreshed rather than frustrated.

Bath time is another perfect time to multi-task. While my little ones bathe, I clean the rest of the bathroom. I admire their beard made of suds or their ability to "swim" in the tub while I tidy and scrub. My kids and I enjoy some laughs together, and the bathroom sparkles! If I'm too tired to clean, I read or make tomorrow's "to-do" list.

While multi-tasking is a mother's best friend, focus is a mom's secret weapon. This may seem contradictory, but the key is knowing when to surrender "doing it all" and focus on who is in front of you. It can be tempting to try to talk to my husband and children at the same time, all while doing the dishes, but I have learned this is not a balancing act worth attempting.

It is a bigger favor to my marriage to stop doing the dishes, ask my children to wait their turn to speak, then face my husband and listen. This tells my husband he is a priority. And besides, he doesn't talk long! The dishes still get done, my husband feels validated, and we both feel closer.

With my children, focus means pausing and really listening whenever they are enthused to tell me something. After school, bedtime, and Sunday dinner are all prime times. This small investment of time and attention is a huge investment in our relationship. The reward is emotional connection that naturally promotes balance.

- Shawnie Sutorius

Children live by their own rhythm, and their tempo often contrasts with ours. Inevitably, it seems when we want to be still and focused, their energy abounds; and when we are rushing to get out the door, they dawdle. I learned early on that trying to dictate my daughter's rhythm usually ended in frustration for us both, so whenever reasonable I take my cues from her and plan my activity around her rhythm.

For me, coordinating my rhythm with my daughter's means being sensitive to the moments that call for closeness and the moments that call for space. As moms, we know when our children need us close and focused. Regardless of their vocabulary, this is one message they manage to get across and one we must not tune out because the rhythm in our own head is playing too loud. The most tender moments I have with my daughter are not ones I have scheduled. They emerge in expressions of openness, sharing, and need that I did not anticipate, but for which I have learned to drop everything to respond and savor. These are the moments when *being* Mom is all that matters.

There are other times when children don't need our full attention; sometimes they just need frequent but intermittent attention. Here, I choose a task that works with what my daughter is doing— throwing in a wash, if she is playing near the laundry room, or cleaning out my wallet, which I can do almost anywhere. Reading separately, but next to each other, is a great way to be together and still do something good for both of us. Cooking together gets dinner made but can also feel like play.

Times when my daughter is content to busy herself for longer stretches are good times to catch up on email, return a phone call, or read an article. I have learned to reserve heavier mental work for times I'm least likely to be interrupted—early mornings, naps, school hours, and after bedtime. And when that isn't enough time, grandparents and other family step in to allow me to get my work done without sacrificing my daughter's need for attention and fun.

However we do it, coordinating our rhythm with that of our family helps everyone feel like they are dancing to the same music. And whether the music calls for *doing* or *being* is less important because truthfully, they both matter—and if we are in tune with the rhythm, most of the time we'll get the steps right too.

Clue # 5: Take Time to Breathe

Everyone who has been on an airplane knows that the cardinal rule of air travel survival is to *"Put on your own oxygen mask first before assisting others."* The logic is simple and sound, in principle at least. Putting it into practice can be harder, but the key is to remember it is not impossible, selfish, or frivolous. It is essential. Without maintaining our own air supply, we are not much use to anyone.

Likewise, taking good care of you is the first step to taking good care of your family. Yes, parenting might just be the most selfless endeavor imaginable, but it doesn't mean that as parents we don't still have needs. In fact, given the dramatic increase in "output" that motherhood demands, our "intake" has to increase significantly, just to keep up!

This mom shares her less-than-successful attempt at "Me-free" motherhood:

> *Immediately after my daughter was born, the nurse cornered my husband, and in her heavy European accent said, "Now, you need to give your wife at least two hours a day all to herself . . . no baby. She will do much better emotionally and mentally with her recovery." My husband agreed, and to his credit he tried to follow her advice, but I made it difficult. After waiting fifteen years to become a mother, I wasn't about to miss a single minute of motherhood! Two hours a day away from my baby seemed like too much to bear.*

For the first two years of my daughter's life, I was there for every moment and milestone. I didn't miss a smile, a scrape, or a tear. But somewhere in my daughter's third year I started to run down. I was tired, cranky, and felt like I had lead weights attached to my feet. Two doctors gave me the same diagnosis . . . too much time taking care of others and not enough time taking care of myself. I had to put myself on my to-do list.

One doctor gave me the assignment to identify things I was doing that were "Good for Me" and "Not Good for Me." The intention was to help me realize what brings me joy so that I could do more of those things and less of what doesn't.

That proved harder than it sounded. Exhausted as I was, I didn't know how to take time for me without missing out on precious experiences with my daughter. How does one be a mother and person at the same time? Turns out I had a long list in the "Not Good for Me" column and not much on the "Good for Me" side. I couldn't even remember what I used to love to do. It took a few days but I slowly rediscovered my likes and interests and dreams . . . on paper at least.

Then came the hard part—doing it. I started eliminating things that were not good for me and replacing them with things that were good for me. This required better time management, planning, and commitment, but the rewards came so quickly that it was worth it. I started blocking out time to read a book, then took on bigger things like taking a class. I took time to reflect and plan what I wanted to accomplish that week. I made myself a priority again, this time understanding that developing myself and my talents is not selfish; what is selfish is to not develop and share them with others.

I still struggle to put myself on the list, but my priorities are in order now, and I am a better mother for it. I have more energy, and I am finding genuine joy in motherhood again. I can't wait until my daughter has her first baby so I can give her this same advice... It will give me a great excuse to be able to hold my beautiful grandbaby for a couple of hours each day!

- Stephanie McKinnon

There is no one formula for how much time moms should spend on themselves and how much on their kids. Making that decision is a matter of conscience, principle, instinct, and circumstance. But this much is for sure—the answer is never just one or the other—my children or me. The well being of one depends on the well being of the other.

It is up to each of us to make "me" time happen and to use it well. I feel more content if I start and end my day with a few minutes alone to read and think quietly. As much as I cherish sleep, losing a few minutes on either side of the day is worth it to have that time to reflect, process, and plan. I also feel better when I allow myself time to exercise, touch base with family and friends, read the news, and take time to do my hair. Even small indulgences can breathe new life into us.

Deciding when we want "me" time and how to best use it is the first step. Otherwise we risk squandering precious free time—leaving us further behind and more out of touch with ourselves. "Me" time can be frivolous or productive, depending on the degree to which it is intentional. Filling those moments with something that feeds our soul will leave us feeling replenished, energized, and better able to give.

Clue #6: Keep on Pedaling

At some point along my journey, balance stopped being a destination at which I hoped to "arrive." The fact that balancing on a bicycle requires constant motion should remind us that there is no end state at which we will finally "be" a balanced person. Living in a perpetual state of balance is not possible, and no one feels balanced all the time. Besides that, pressuring ourselves to maintain constant balance only adds one more layer of stress to our already-full plate.

More often than not, life is messy, disorderly, inconvenient, and overwhelming. We don't always have control over the external pushes and pulls in our lives. Deadlines loom and responsibilities pile up. Life's daily demands and mishaps can make us feel like we are pedaling furiously, but getting nowhere fast.

Sometimes it's whatever we are doing to meet the pressing demands of the day that amounts to balancing appropriately. There are days I pedal from early morning to late at night and don't feel much farther ahead than the day before. (And in truth, sometimes I'm not.) But I am better off because I stayed in motion, keeping balance with whatever that day threw at me.

Finding the right fit for all the things we value is not easy, but it's more apt to happen when we keep trying anyway. It helps to remember that day-to-day balance is different from overall balance. In every mom's life, some days are just plain crazy, and merely getting through the day is all we can do. But when our lives (overall) are balanced, we can weather those days much easier, knowing that today's headwind will pass, and we'll be riding in better conditions tomorrow.

This is not to say we can't stop once in a while to look back at where we've come from, take in the scenery, and plan our route going forward—as long as we get back on the bike each time.

We find balance as we keep pedaling in the direction of the things that matter most, today and in the long run—remembering that not every leg of our journey through motherhood is a graceful progression. Sometimes we hit a rock or get a leg cramp or ride in circles. The point is to keep pedaling anyway, not just to reach a destination, but for the adventure and growth we get along the way.

Clue #7: Enjoy the Ride

To push the bicycle metaphor even further, pedaling to stay balanced does not mean racing to keep up with unrealistic expectations. Sure, there are difficult stretches of pedaling uphill, but there are also times of coasting across plateaus and racing downhill laughing. And we can always slow down when we're tired, get a push when we need one, and, of course, pause to watch a sunset. Wherever we are in our journey, eventually we realize the ride is what it's all about.

Enjoying the ride is not to imply that everything about motherhood is enjoyable. Sick kids, for example, are not fun. Potty training—also not fun. Last-minute book reports, enforcing rules, and cell phones in the toilet, multiple times—still not fun. And the list goes on. But in the big scheme of things, the reality is that being a mom should *and honestly can* be fun MOST of the time.

If you advertised a paying job where co-workers had even half the personality and attributes of children (funny, playful, imaginative, spontaneous, wise, honest, sincere, and even cute!) who wouldn't apply for that job? Children are inherently fun. They say hilarious things when you least expect it and you never know what they're going to do next (I think half the time they surprise themselves!).

My daughter had a phase in which she loved playing with spray bottles full of water. She'd spray anything that stood still (that kept the cat on her toes). One day a family member let out a scream from across the house, followed by "Oh Anina!" I looked at my daughter for an explanation, to which she responded frankly, "I didn't do it. And I didn't do it with the spray bottle. And I won't do it again." Turned out she'd made her daily rounds with the spray bottle, saturating all the toilet seats in the house. Needless to say, it made for a fun surprise to the user.

Granted, there's no escaping work, in life or in motherhood—it's in every pile in every corner and in every cry for help—but it doesn't have to be drudgery. The more we make our work also our pleasure, the less we'll fret over the pursuit of balance, or anything else, for that matter!

We can look at motherhood as mostly work and stress, with an occasional reprieve on Mother's Day and when our kids are sleeping, or we can decide that being a mom is a pretty great gig that has a few rough patches, but overall is a lot of fun!

Putting the Pieces in Place

No prescription for balance works every day or for every person. Like solving a puzzle, we try a piece here and a piece there until one looks and feels right in a certain place. So it is for me with the clues I have collected thus far—they are the puzzle pieces that help me bridge the gaps and round out the borders of a life almost full to overflowing. They are, to use Lindbergh's words, what help me to remain whole and balanced, despite whatever forces attempt to pull me off center.

Living a balanced life is a lifelong process of striving for the ideal while keeping our expectations real. It helps to remember that we are modeling for our children how to have a balanced life, and that includes being honest about our struggles, as well as our successes.

Talking with them about how we choose what things to devote time to and why, helps them understand that what we give our time to reflects what we value most. Showing them that we value work *and* play, social time *and* personal time, service to others *and* developing our own talents, gives them a broader picture of what it means to be a well-rounded person. It also teaches them that balance, while not a perfect science, is more about choices and attitude than circumstance and chance.

We are the architects of our lives and our time. With our hearts focused on those we love and the things we value, we can have the wisdom to choose what matters most, the flexibility to revise our choices when necessary, the determination to keep pedaling no matter what life throws at us, and the enthusiasm to make the ride fun for ourselves and our families!

Sarah Turner is a wife to one great husband and a mother to six children, four boys and two girls, between the ages of 17 and brand new (her baby girl was born right when this book was going to press!). That means she is doing middle-of-the-night feedings, driving lessons, and everything in between—all in a day's work.

She strives to raise her children using old-fashioned values and tries as hard as she can to live a simpler, slower, family-based life, and to keep her kids young in a world that wants them to grow up too fast.

She loves babies, staying home, clean floors, writing, photography, good books, and orderly piles of laundry. Sarah considers the role as mother the most important vocation on earth. She blogs about it all at memoriesoncloverlane.blogspot.com.

CHAPTER EIGHT

HAVE A DEEPER YES
The Power of Priorities

by Sarah Turner

Keep Your Head On

When I was young, my dad experimented with raising chickens. We had ten hens and one noisy rooster. The fun lasted until that inevitable day when it was time to fill our freezer with poultry. My dad did the messy work while my sisters and I hid in our rooms. If I had peeked, I would have seen for myself the true meaning of the expression "running around like a chicken with its head cut off."

Fast forward many years later, and I know exactly what this expression means. As a mother to five, I am managing a household, volunteering at school, renovating our home, helping at church, and anything else that is thrown on my plate. I often look like a chicken with her head cut off—running in every direction but going nowhere, stressed out, and desperately needing a pause or reset button.

One day, while skimming the local paper, I came across a particularly long and impressive obituary. From the picture, I expected a prominent woman with a long list of accolades, awards, and achievements. Instead, I found a heartfelt letter written to a mother by her children. It spoke of her dedication and commitment to raising her family. Little things like her smile, her fresh baked goodies, and her love for life were meaningful to them. This is how they would always remember her. Plus they shared funny stories, like the time she let her boys keep their catch from a fishing trip in the bathtub when they couldn't bear to cook their new friends for dinner. They spoke of the joy she found in her chosen vocation as a mother, her constant presence, and her calm, reliable, and loving spirit. The letter brought to light what a dynamic person she was to her children.

The obituary moved me to tears. All day long it weighed heavily on my mind. I was deeply touched at the purposeful life she had led, and I wondered whether I was living life the way I wanted, or simply surviving the life I was lucky to have?

I sat down and answered a couple vital questions—questions that were hard, but gave me important insight into what kind of woman I wanted to be. I asked myself the following: What is important to me? How do I want my children and husband to describe me one day? How will people remember me? I certainly did not want to be remembered as a chicken running around with her head cut off!

The questions kept coming. What do I want to contribute to this world? What do I like to do? What makes me happy? What am I good at? What do I not like to do? Could I make those things go away? If I couldn't, could I make them easier and less time consuming?

I decided to make choices and decisions from that time on that brought me closer to the person I wanted to be.

Answering these tough questions helped me determine the kind of spirit I wanted to exude for the rest of my life. Then I established priorities to make it happen.

Sometimes we get so caught up in surviving the pressures of the day, being pushed and pulled in every direction, that days, months, and even years can pass without making time to think about how we are being perceived by those around us. I wondered if my children saw me as present and available or always occupied with something else. I thought about how I was often preoccupied during conversations with my husband, thinking of the next thing I had to do. Was I giving my best to those I love, or was I making them feel like an entry on my to-do list? I realized that if I didn't establish principles and specific priorities to guide me through deciding what to do and getting through the chaotic days, the chaos would define me.

Examine Your Life

After some deep thinking, I wrote down all my responsibilities and commitments and realized I was going in too many directions—stretching myself way too thin. I wasn't enjoying anything I was doing. I was only trying to get the task completed so I could get on to the next item in my never-ending list.

I lacked passion and focus. I wasn't engaged or enthusiastic. I lacked the very qualities I admired in others. Instead of pride, fulfillment, and the sense of "a job well done," I just felt guilty.

While completing a project, I was feeling guilty about not spending time with my children. I would zip through the project quickly, but once the project was completed, I did not feel proud of the work I rushed through. While I was spending the days with my children, I would be tense and anxious to get to my work later that evening, which would leave me feeling guilty for not being fully present with my children. I would fall into bed almost every evening feeling like I never gave anything my best.

This discovery required me to be brave. Change is hard, and everyone in the family is affected by it. I knew from the soul searching I had done; I needed to make my actual life look closer to the one I desired.

At the time, I was running a successful decorative painting business—a business I operated only at times that did not interfere with being a mom (nights, weekends, nap time). My husband and I decided that we were both willing to make some changes so I could feel like the mom, wife, and woman I wanted to be. We decided I would walk away from my business.

The extra income earned was not worth the mental toll it was taking on me. Every bit of time spent away from my family was spent concentrating on my business. I needed time to recharge through exercise, reading, or spending time alone with my thoughts. It was hard at first to say no to clients when they wanted me for a job. I didn't want to disappoint them. But I found it is much easier to say no when you know WHY you are saying no.

Surprisingly, I was actually giddy after the first "no". It was fun! It was freeing! A "no" to one thing, was a "yes" to something else, and I was thrilled at what I was saying yes to.

Over the years, I've become quite confident at saying no. At first, I would follow the word "no" with a long explanation—which made me sound foolish. Then my mom advised me to simply say "No, it doesn't work for my family. " That's IT. Period. It is absolutely truthful, and how can anyone argue with it?

Matthew Kelly, the author of *Building Better Families*, writes, "We give our time to who and what we love. Children yearn for the time of their parents. In a world where we are pulled in so many directions, finding the time to spend with our children is perhaps the greatest challenge facing parents today. That is why it is so important to know what matters most and what we really are about. The only way to say no to something is to have a deeper yes. We have to constantly assert that spending time with our children is a deeper yes. Otherwise, we will be accosted on a daily basis and carried away from our families by the seemingly urgent things. There are many urgent things in our lives each day, but the most important things are hardly ever urgent. That's why we need to identify them, give them priority, and place them at the center of our lives."

Assess and Reassess

Over time, I began to realize the process of establishing priorities is continuous. It's NOT a one-time question-and-answer session. Reassessing priorities is a life-long endeavor. As soon as we think we have control over our lives or discover the meaning of the word "happiness," something completely unexpected seems to come along. Such is life.

Learning to anticipate change is important. Besides the usual big changes, like moving into a new home, starting a new job, or pregnancy, there are also changes in family dynamics. Ages and stages of children make them needier at certain times than others. Having an infant with colic, a defiant toddler, or a teenager testing the boundaries are all intense times for mothers.

I find the best way to prioritize during times of change is to remember that less is more. After the arrival of a newborn, for example, I make it a rule to remember to say no to absolutely everything. I expect to be in pure survival mode for that first year, so I go easy on myself. If my children are clean and fed, I have had a successful day.

Know Your Threshold

Another lesson I've learned in establishing priorities is to be in tune with my personal stress threshold. When I feel overwhelmed, snappy, and exhausted, and the spirit I want to exude is NOT what

I am displaying, I know it is time to take a step back. Knowing and accepting your tipping point and staying under it is vital.

When my daughter was in first grade, I volunteered to be a Daisy Scout co-leader for her classroom. I shared leadership duties with another mom I really admired. She seemed to gracefully pull off everything she was involved in. By the second week, I knew I was in trouble. A weekly meeting with twenty-five girls was hard enough, but I also had to keep track of my busy three-year-old and entertain his bored eight-year-old brother. On top of that, I was in the heart of my first trimester of pregnancy, constantly nauseated and exhausted.

Meanwhile the other leader was SO into it, soaking up her role with joy. I felt guilty for not enjoying it like she did. I went home every week feeling completely depleted, with a headache from that dark church basement and three whining, hungry children. I'd get a late start on dinner, I would snap at the kids, and I would barely look at my husband when he walked in the door. Daisy Scouts was stressing us all out, and the kicker was, at the end of the year, my daughter told me she didn't really want to join in the first place.

It was a great lesson for me. I realized I needed to be aware of my stress threshold and not expect it to match anyone else's. We all have different goals, strengths and weaknesses. Volunteering is an important aspect of parenting and a great way to be present in your child's life. But it is best to volunteer in an area you truly enjoy and are passionate about, and when the timing is right for your family.

Identify the Purpose

I also learned to keep in mind the purpose of my priority list. Today more than ever, we have so many choices and opportunities for our families and ourselves. Asking myself the question, "What is the PURPOSE of this?"—whether it's a volunteer position, children's lesson or activity, or something personal for me—helps me determine the worth of an activity. I try to select experiences that offer some level of fulfillment—for the mind, spirit, or body.

Katrina Kenison, author of *Mitten Strings for God*, writes, "So often we do things because we think we should, or for fear of being judged or left out if we don't, or because everyone else is doing them, or because our children want to sample every new activity they hear their friends talking about. But how good it feels to release ourselves from the 'should' and to tune in to a different rhythm. To do things just for the fun of it. To have a life that is rich but not rushed, happy but not hectic."

Don't Forget Yourself

Mothers truly are the spirit of the home, and sometimes it's a mighty undertaking. Our moods, our inner integrity, and the tone we set in our homes, are reflected in each of our children's eyes. We owe it to them, and to ourselves, to thoughtfully nurture strength of spirit, or we'll struggle to create a graceful and harmonious life.

One of my favorite quotes says,

"They may forget what you said, but they will never forget how you made them feel." - Carl Buechner

Being a mother is BIG work. It fills our hearts and minds quickly, and no matter where we find ourselves in the journey of motherhood, we need to leave time to replenish ourselves. We must put ourselves among the first items on the priority list, no matter how uncomfortable that might make us feel. Caring for ourselves gives us the ability to offer our families the best we have.

Make Sure it Matters

"How we spend our days is, of course, how we spend our lives."
- Annie Dillard

The years raising children fly by at warp speed. My tiny firstborn infant that once was swimming in his newborn-sized pajamas is now wearing men's size eleven basketball shoes. Before I know it, my sweet little daughter who loved to play dress-up with my ancient prom dresses, will soon be shopping for one of her own. While we are raising our children, we are growing and changing too.

Life is too precious to live without intention.

I want to be able to say that I lived my days consciously, knowing that I placed motherhood at the forefront, but that I also followed my passions, used my talents, and did my best to make choices that allowed me to live with clarity, purpose and a sense of calmness to days. I want to give a deep yes to the things that really matter.

* * * * *

Saying No

During a few moments of introspection, I realized the majority of my yeses are being given away to people outside my family, and even fewer are being given to me. But if saying yes to my family and myself is first, then the nos seem to come much easier.

Everyday I need to have time with God, be creative in some way, have a slot of time that isn't scheduled, and spend time with my kids and my husband that isn't rushed. These aren't grand things, but they're important to me and help bring a sense of calm to my world.

They're also things I never really knew about myself—or maybe I did, but I was just too busy to take notice.

Either way, I now see that the outcome of not giving myself these simple basics is that I start to make decisions for all the wrong reasons. That's just not an option for me anymore. I can't be the kind of person I want to be when I'm living that way.

I'm sure there will be times when I will struggle with the fact that saying no will benefit our family, especially when it's a difficult answer to give, but I'm ready for the challenge. I'll remind myself that by saying no, I can live at a slower pace and enjoy what's in front of me. I'll think about how saying no is helping me to teach my kids to do the same for themselves one day. But mostly I'm going to choose to say no to a few things so I can say yes to what's important.

- Heather Hamilton

An Overpriced Spatula

Last year, I went to a cooking show party—the kind of party where you go and enjoy a demonstration and some food, and have the opportunity to buy something used in the demonstration.

This particular party fell on a very busy night. My husband was due to leave for scout camp early the next day, but that night he went straight to bed with strep throat. My girlfriend had just left with her daughters after we'd spent the day working on projects together while our eight kids played. My kitchen floor was in desperate need of being swept.

Material scraps, loose threads, and snack crumbs were everywhere. The slip-n-slide and wet towels lay limply, waiting to be put away.

Dinner dishes scattered the counter. My children, over-stimulated from the day in the sun, desperately needed some settling down. My two-month old baby needed feeding. My phone kept ringing with an over-eager friend calling to tell me that Michael Jackson had died.

It was time to head out to the party, but I didn't want to go. I didn't have the energy to go. I didn't have the time to go. I didn't really have money in my budget to go. But I had an obligation. "I was invited, and I need to support this lady," I thought.

So I went, and the party consisted of me, the host, and the cooking show presenter. I felt a great sigh of relief at my presence and thought, "What if I hadn't come? No one would be here. I have to buy something now that I am the only guest here!"

Despite my jumbled thoughts, the party began. I knew that chaos was ensuing at home, but how could I leave this "one dish, black-bean chicken" demonstration without appearing rude? After all, I was the only guest! So I stayed. I watched. I taste tested. And I bought.

Two hours later and twenty dollars poorer, I entered my home. My kitchen and family room looked like a bomb had gone off. My children all began to talk at once about who did what to whom. My tired and sickly husband sat there attempting to comfort a cranky two-month old baby. With one quick announcement I said, "I just spent twenty dollars on a spatula." My polite and ever-supportive husband simply responded, "Dumb."

"But," I continued, "The money was well worth it, because I am committing now to never again go to a party like that when there are other things I really need to be doing."

As I lay in bed that night, I did some self-evaluation. I thought about my earlier declaration, "The money was well worth it, because I am committing now to never again go to a party like that." I pondered the consequences of my decision. My home, my children, my husband, and a baby desperately needed me, yet I couldn't let down a lady in my neighborhood? Something was amiss. My priorities were not aligned.

Thanks to that twenty-dollar spatula, things have changed in my life. Every invitation, request, or obligation that invites me to leave my home is now carefully considered. I ask myself, "How will me being away from home benefit me or my family?" That night, I didn't go to the party to come back a better person. I didn't go to serve. I didn't go to set an example for my children. I didn't go to relax, have a good time, or come home rejuvenated. I didn't go to spend time with a family member. I didn't go to lift and inspire another. I went because I felt obligated to someone else.

Not anymore.

I use that spatula frequently—it happens to be my favorite in the utensil drawer. I've used it to cook some wonderful meals, desserts, and treats my family has enjoyed. But the spatula came at a price. A price, I can now say, I was happy to pay. Twenty dollars might seem expensive for a spatula, but the lesson learned was priceless.

- **Tiffany Sowby**

First Things First

Lying on the floor next to my two-year-old one afternoon, I watched her play. As she tried to stuff an armful of items into a bucket, she became frustrated that they kept overloading and falling out. I reached over. "Here, Sweetheart," I said. "Let's try this." Slowly, I helped her pull the items out of the bucket. "Let's put the biggest things in first, then the little things in next." She watched with satisfaction as we fit everything in. I smiled inwardly, knowing I was teaching a true principle.

The irony, of course, was that I had not followed that principle myself at all that day. I sighed. It seemed I'd been getting nothing accomplished since the moment my infant cried at 5:00 a.m. I was running around trying to mark off my to-do list, but feeling more frustrated than fulfilled. I knew it was because I had not started the day with the "first-things-first" mentality.

C.S. Lewis once said, "When first things are put first, second things are not suppressed but increased." I love that truism. When I put the most important things first, which for me means taking time to turn inward spiritually, the rest of things in my day come into focus more clearly and are done with more patience, more stride and more love.

- Kristi Linton

Wearing Too Many Hats

Sometimes my life gets busy. Too busy. I allow myself to be distracted by too many things. I hear myself saying to the kids several times a week, "Look, you're just going to have to wait a minute." Or, "I don't have time to talk to you about that right now." And, "I want to help you with that but I just can't."

When I start talking like that to my kids, things need to change. The change that needs to happen is with me.

Usually, the problem is that I am wearing too many hats. I am so good at taking on new hats that I end up like The Cat in the Hat from Dr. Seuss. You know the story. Here is little cat A, B, C, D . . . all the way up to Z. Yep, I allow myself to get to the stage where I feel like I am wearing the whole alphabet.

When this happens, drastic action is needed, and I give myself a day off. I take off my hats. No friend hat, no cleaning hat, no gym hat, no blogging hat (man was that one hard to take off for the day), and no chef hat. I decide to just wear my mummy hat for the day.

At first it is hard, but then I feel as if a weight has been lifted off my shoulders, and I feel a real relief.

My goal for the day becomes to just "hang out" at home with the kids.

I watch the kids play, and I sit outside and talk with them. Really talk with them. I listen and love everything they share. They have such cute little ideas and ways of expressing themselves. It becomes a wonderful day, just wearing my 'Mummy Hat'.

- Naomi Ellis

Spinning Plates

I once heard someone compare the way we manage our lives to spinning plates. I can relate to that. A man gets plates spinning, one at a time, atop thin poles, until he has multiple plates spinning and must run from plate to plate to keep each one going before the momentum slows and each plate falls, shattering to the ground. After hearing this analogy, I took a good look at my priorities. I chose several "plates" I thought were worth spinning and tended to them carefully.

And then . . . we had twins.

The news that we were expecting not just our fourth, but also our fifth child, was met with delight and some trepidation. One mother of twins said to me, "Keep this in mind: if it doesn't directly affect your children, it doesn't matter." I thought, "Everything I do directly affects my children! What could I possibly let go of that wouldn't affect my children?" I started to panic. I looked again at my priorities, but I couldn't let anything go . . . not yet. So I kept spinning those plates, secretly believing I could keep them all going—even with twins.

The twins were born six weeks early and with mild complications. Within a few weeks, we welcomed them joyfully into our home. The plates began to slow. My husband brought home dinner and searched for clean socks. My nine-year-old daughter wondered if I'd ever be able to hug her with both arms again or if I'd always be holding a baby. Six-year-old Mack showed signs of insecurity, including compulsive hand-washing and a heart-breaking fear of germs. My arms ached to hold my three-year-old daughter. School started. We forgot homework and show-and-tell. I didn't volunteer. The house was a mess. I braced myself and waited for the plates to shatter all around me.

Then I discovered a secret. Most of the plates I kept spinning were paper plates. When I stopped tending to them, they slowed and gradually stopped spinning. They fell to the ground, but quietly and almost uneventfully. And I realized they would wait there until I could pick them up and get them spinning again.

The panic subsided, and I looked to the plates that were still spinning, and they were precious. They represented each of my family members. "Dave" rather than "Dave's laundry." "Grace" not "Grace's homework." "Mack" and not even "Mack's fears." Now, self-assured, I could assure each family member that I would not let them fall. This season would pass, and we would be better for it.

The twins are now sixteen months. Many of those paper plates are spinning again. The laundry still piles up, but most of the homework gets done. I volunteer in the classrooms and go on field trips. We breathe a collective sigh of relief, and we know better how to love and lift each other. I even make dinner almost every night. But we still eat on—you guessed it—paper plates.

- Marcie Richards

Saren and her husband, Jared, had five kids in five years, which wasn't exactly planned. In fact, Saren has learned that very little about motherhood (or life in general) goes as planned!

After growing up all over the place (Washington DC, London, Salt Lake City, Mexico, Japan, Boston) as the oldest of the nine children of best-selling parenting authors, Richard and Linda Eyre, Saren graduated from Wellesley College, got her M.Ed. at Harvard, and conducted training conferences for educators across the country. But it wasn't until after she got married and had kids that the real education and hard work began! In response to what SHE needed as a mom and her desire to use her background in training and development to help other moms, Saren worked with April Perry to found The Power of Moms.

When she's not trying to answer five different needs and questions at once, Saren squeezes in all the reading, traveling, hiking, and biking she can. For more information, visit Saren's blog, Five Kids in Five Years, which is found at looslifamily.blogspot.com.

CHAPTER NINE

BEGIN WITH THE END IN MIND
The Power of Organization

by Saren Eyre Loosli

Organizing is what you do before you do something, so that when you do it, it is not all mixed up. - A. A. Milne

Should I really be writing this chapter? There are so many moms I know who are vastly more organized than I am. But as I've thought long and hard about organization, I've realized a lot of important things for myself that I hope will help you as well.

Organization means different things to different people. I have a friend who keeps her house spotless and clutter-free but somehow can't find anything she needs when she needs it (out of sight out of mind?). I have another friend who doesn't carry a planner or use a calendar but very seldom forgets things and gets her five children on time to all their activities and special events.

My husband feels he's organized if he can find what he's looking for immediately—and somehow he can do that quite well even when his stuff in the garage or papers on his desk look like a huge mess to me. I feel like I'm *not* organized if there are any papers out on my desk or non-food-related items on my kitchen counter tops. And my brain feels like a mess if I don't make my weekly list of "immediate actions" and refer to them each morning as I get going.

Here's how family "organization" works for one mom:

Hubby: "Has anyone seen my shoes?"

Me: "Under the table."

Hubby: "Which one?"

Me: "The end table where they were kicked under, like always."

Hubby: "How about my keys?"

Me: "Downstairs on the arm of the couch."

Hubby: "My phone?"

Me: "Stuck between couch cushions in the living room."

Hubby: "Wait, what about my wallet?"

Me: "You left it in the console of your Jeep."

Hubby: "Oh yeah. Has anyone seen my hat?"

Are you KIDDING me? Thank goodness I adore this man.

I live a life of organized chaos. We're a fun-loving family that stays very busy—a family of four with two Chihuahuas and a rotating door that invites house guests at all times of the year. My kids are creative and inventive—which naturally leads to some messes. Most of the time, the chaos is fun.

My ultimate goal is to simplify our lives by having everything organized. This would mean that everything has a place, the closets are perfectly organized and labeled, my books and files are where I left them in my office, bills pay themselves, and shoes can find their own way to the closets.

I've since come to my senses and I am settling for being able to see the kitchen counters and not get anything stuck to my feet when I walk through living room. Yes, it's not my idea of "clean and organized," but as long as others are helping out, I've decided to not be such a perfectionist.

This brings me to the chore list. Sometimes it gets done, sometimes it doesn't, but mom's rule is that if it's not done before I get home from work, you don't get allowance for that day. This tends to work with my ten-year-old, and I'm hoping it rubs off on the seven-year-old soon. However, she tends to be a walking tornado . . . things literally fall on the floor as she walks by. I'm thinking about having her tested for a sixth sense. Isn't that what they call it when you can make things move without touching them?

At least with a system of chores (written down and posted on the fridge counts as a system, right?) and some family members that help, we can typically find the things we need to make our family function without too much freaking out—on good days. This is what I call My Life of Organized Chaos.

Now, who has my pedometer and why is the dog in the baby doll stroller?

- Chantól Sego

As these examples show, there's no one right way to be organized and no one way that organization should look, but I feel pretty confident saying that organization is important to all of us. When we feel organized, it's easier to get things done, to find things and to feel that our life is generally under control.

Why be Organized?

Before delving into the "hows" of organization (much of which is offered through the excellent Power of Moms *Mind Organization for Moms* and *Family Systems* programs), it's pretty darn important to stop and think about the "whys" of organization. What do you personally crave when it comes to organization? What areas of your life feel most disorganized? What is not particularly organized in your life but doesn't really matter that much to you?

Perhaps you could take a few minutes to think about or jot down your responses to the questions above before you move on. Then as you read the rest of this chapter, record any sparks of inspiration that will help you move toward the type of organized life you'd like to live.

In general, organization is a means to an end, not an end. There are some "organization junkies" out there who love to organize for the sheer joy of it, but for most people, organization is something we do because it provides us with something else we really value. When we think about the "end" that we're organizing towards, we can better assess how much and what kind of organization is really important for us.

So why be organized? Here's what I came up with:

- So we can find things that we need in a timely manner and not lose things that are important.
- So we can enjoy the present without our brain constantly being distracted by schedule items and tasks we need to remember, ideas and worries that haven't been dealt with, or piles of stuff that remind us of undone tasks.
- So we can get things done on a daily and weekly basis (and help our family members with the things they need to get done).

- So we can raise our children in a deliberate manner and help them develop the traits and abilities we know they need.
- So we can steadily work towards our longer-term goals that tie to our values, dreams and deeply-felt passions and purposes.

Based on the purposes of organization above, here are some areas of organization that every mom can use some help with (especially me!). I'll go through each of these areas in the rest of this chapter:

- Thing Organization
- Thought and Task Organization
- Time and Routine Organization
- Family Organization

Thing Organization

If you're like me, the first thing that pops into my head when I hear the word "organization" is displaying a clean house. My father used to prep us for chores by saying, "Today we're going to move the house to the left a couple of inches." Lately, I've been finding that statement too true for my own comfort.

It seems like I get up, my children move things around, and I must move them to the right or left in an effort to find order. I used to want my house clean throughout the whole day. I found I was cleaning up the same messes three or four times a day. My latest and more realistic goal is to have the house clean and orderly at least once a day. After all, I am outnumbered. My children and my husband un-do everything I do faster than I can do it.

There's a saying that says, "Cleaning the house while the children are still growing is like shoveling the walks while it is still snowing." Cleaning is an endless process and often menial in nature. It definitely has its place, though. A clean environment helps us stay healthy and safe both physically and emotionally.

- Sharla Olsen

For most of us, as the saying goes, "thing order precedes thought order." Our minds generally feel cluttered when our homes are overly cluttered for our comfort level, but each of us has a different level of comfort with clutter and cleanliness. Perfectionism is bound to be a losing battle when it comes to keeping our homes neat and clean with kids underfoot. But it's important to think about what matters most to us and discard ideas that others may have passed along that actually don't resonate to us personally. I've adopted my friend April's basic standards for my home: "clean enough to be healthy, messy enough to be happy" and "clean enough to be sanitary, messy enough to be sane."

Following are some tips and ideas I've figured out and gathered from others that can help us with "Thing Organization" in our homes.

Keep the "Stuff" Quantity Under Control

Downsizing your "stuff" is an important key to clutter control. Having moved every few years my whole life and having helped many other people complete moves, I've seen that having lots of stuff is never a positive thing and can be a real problem. I've helped people pack up houses full of over-saved mementos, seldom-used or outdated electronic gadgets, mismatched dishes, out-dated and out-grown clothes, and broken items that "I might get fixed or need someday." I've seen how people end up needing storage units and larger homes to accommodate their ever-increasing piles of stuff. It's so easy to accumulate in our society. So many things are relatively cheap, and buying things is pretty much a national pastime.

Here are a few rules of thumb you may want to live by if you want to minimize the "stuff" in your life and make organization easier:

178

- **"If in doubt, throw it out."** There are so many things we keep because we think there's a slight chance of needing them again. But there's a far greater chance we WON'T need that thing again. And if you do happen to need it down the road, it's probably not that big a deal to get another one. So get rid of it! We keep important official documents and throw away pretty much all other papers (or we avoid even receiving papers—most bills and correspondence can be handled in a paperless way these days). When it comes to all the "special" things my kids create, most of them get thrown out too—but only after they've had a place of honor on the bulletin board for a while, they've been properly photographed, and the digital photo has been added to that child's "special things" folder on the computer that they can review any time. They do keep a handful of their "most" special things in hard-copy form, and these go into sheet protectors in their own binder (we create a binder for every three years that contains these most special things).

- **When something comes in, something must go out.** If you buy something new, or if your child gets new toys for Christmas or for a birthday, you can make it a general rule that something should be given away to Goodwill or to a younger cousin or friend—or thrown away in the case of things that are shabby or broken—in exchange.

- **Embrace an "abundance" mentality.** Sometimes we hold onto things because we paid good money for them, but we don't even really like or need them anymore. Rather than embracing this "scarcity" mentality, embrace the "abundance" mentality. We all have more than we need. We don't need all that we have. Giving is a pleasure. And giving away something that is still perfectly usable can make someone else really happy.

- **Think of toys and clothes as consumables** (like food, toilet paper or tickets to a movie). There are some heirloom toys and clothes we may want to save for posterity. But in general, if you think of toys and clothes as regular consumable parts of life that you'll use and then pass along or throw away when they've been outgrown or aren't particularly used anymore, it's easier to get rid of them. If you pay $10 for a toy and your children really enjoy it for a month and then it's just taking up space, just think of that $10 like you'd think of the $10 you spent to go to a movie or go bowling. It was money well spent because it provided nice enjoyment for a period of time, but just like you don't have to keep the movie ticket stubs, you don't have to keep the toy. It can be passed along to someone else who might really enjoy it.

- **Have a "giveaway box" on hand all the time and use that trashcan freely.** *"I routinely keep a charity donation box that fills up as I find things that have out-lived their usefulness around our home. My favorite aid to downsizing is my trashcan. I use whichever method fits the moment and item in question. It's empowering!" - Sharla Olsen*

Decrease Stress by having a Place for Everything

One mom writes,

I love to organize. I know it may sound crazy—but I do. Give me a stuffed closet or a disheveled toy room and I am good to go. I am not sure exactly where this trait comes from, but it is actually quite annoying on many occasions. Don't get me wrong, I spend plenty of my time playing with the kids and taking out toys, but in the back of my mind is always the thought of organizing them in some better way.

I don't function well in chaos. My home is fairly tidy, but not always clean. What is my secret? My motto is: "Everything has a place." Many moms get discouraged with the toys, shoes, clothes, bills, etc. lying around their homes. One reason it gets so mind boggling is that these things don't have a place. When everything in our homes has a place, we are better able to organize and function.

We can't ask our children to put away their school bags and shoes if there is not a place for them. And, shouldn't that place be somewhere really handy to the door they use to come in and out of the house? We don't have a fancy mudroom, but each kid has a hook in our entryway for coats and backpacks with space on the floor beneath for shoes. When I ask my kids to clean these things up, they know right where to put them.

Each toy needs a place. That doesn't mean that during playtime my home is not littered with toys in every nook and cranny. However, when clean-up time comes, the kids know where everything goes. Try a bookshelf for larger items, a plastic tote for cars or a cute basket for baby toys. Too many toys? Put some away for a while and rotate them periodically or donate some to charity.

As moms, we need to be logical as to where we put these "places." There has to be a spot close to the front door for shoes (a simple shoe rack can work). Our children are not going to go to their rooms each time and put their shoes in their closets when they come in the door—and having them run to their rooms to get their shoes when it's time to go somewhere would make us late all the time. You could try keeping socks in a basket near the shoes as well.

Where do we put the mountains of paperwork and mail to go through? There needs to be a place. Try a file or an inbox on your counter or a mail center on your wall near the door. And I find that if I go through the mail right away and use the trash can liberally, my inbox can stay pretty manageable.

My motto has made all of the difference in maintaining order and organization in our home. My husband likes to joke, "Everything has a place—and I know mine!" As long as his shoes and dirty clothes are picked up, all is well!

- Mary Christensen

Thought and Task Organization

So if "thing order precedes thought order," then once we've got the things in our life in order, it's time to get our thoughts in order—and this includes our "to do" lists, our worries, our hopes, our calendar items, our goals—all the things that fill our minds day to day. Different systems work for different people.

Develop a System that Works for You

It's important that we create or tailor a program for time, thought, and task organization to our own unique needs.

The "how" of accomplishing what's most important is the nuts and bolts of being organized as a mom. When it comes right down to it, we need to find something that will help us remember what we need to do.

Remembering is one of the keys to being organized. Choose your own method. Some people have planners or file folders or sticky notes or to-do lists that help them remember everything they need to accomplish for that day. Do whatever works best for you. Each of our situations is different, so what works for one mom won't necessarily work for another mom. When I started out as a mother, I could easily remember the appointments we had

*coming up because I didn't have that many places I had to be.
Then, after having my fifth child, my oldest started school, and I
felt bamboozled for a whole year. It took me awhile to figure out
what I needed to do in order to stay on top of everything. I've
relied heavily on the list system throughout my years as mom.
Now, I require a BIG calendar and a to-do list to keep our
family afloat and headed in the right direction.*

- Sharla Olsen

Thousands of moms have had great success using the Power of
Moms *Mind Organization for Moms* program to help them plan
projects and accomplish goals successfully. It also helps them keep
track of their short- and long-term ideas and dreams, and frees their
minds of worries, calendar items and "to-do" lists so they can really
be "present" for their families. I won't go into the details of Mind
Organization here, but this mom explains a bit about why using
some sort of system for organizing our thoughts, tasks, etc. is so
important:

*I confess to being an overachiever. I feel a perpetual itch to start
new projects and constantly find myself mentally starting lists of
things to buy—at four different stores, debating on what new
recipes to try, scheming a girls' night out, considering tomorrow's
early morning run, plotting my next apartment de-clutter, and
anticipating the book to be read that is waiting by my pillow.
While I do my best to make sure essentials and priorities are at
the top of my list, I proceed to cram all sorts of other things into
the nooks and crannies of my schedule and brain because I
deeply enjoy looking forward to projects and events and getting
things accomplished.*

*To organize all these activities and thoughts, I've always turned
to one of my most favorite and reliable comforts: lists. I love lists.
I love filling a pad of paper with my sprawling handwriting,*

watching the transfer of ideas and thoughts become more concrete. I feel in control and organized when I write things down. My usual solution for organizing things I need to do, want to do, and someday hope to do is simple: I make lists. Nothing is better than making a bold slash through a particularly daunting task item on a long stretch of a "To-do" list.

But when my big long list is jam-packed and overflowing with information, ideas, tasks, and deadlines (self-imposed and actual), I can get overwhelmed. As with many good things in life, too much of anything can be detrimental. Occasionally (okay, to be more honest I should say regularly), I found that my once-refreshing list system was becoming never-ending and overwhelming. Plus I realized that I have priorities such as personal worship, time with my husband, unstructured time with my girls, family playtime, downtime for myself, and sleep that weren't making it on my lists and were being neglected.

Recently I was thrilled—absolutely floored—when I discovered the Mind Organization for Moms (M.O.M.) system on the Power of Moms website. I consider it epic in my career as a mother, significant in my daily success, and monumental in my happiness. The system literally took me a week to even consider. I will admit the newness was a little daunting. Now that I am a full-fledged believer and implementer, I am still learning to trust and rely on the system. Occasionally I find myself resorting to my previous frantic and hectic norms. When this happens, I recognize how ineffective I was in my former way of handling my tasks, priorities and goals. With a little readjusting, I get back on track.

At one time in my life I was a slave to my "to-do" list. I often told myself that I could play and rest once everything was done. Unfortunately, a mother's work is never done. Daily, I set out to conquer my un-prioritized lists, attacking each item with frenzy, never considering the time or energy I had available. Initially it was rewarding to tick items off my list but it was exhausting to keep up the pace. I survived but didn't thrive. I commonly felt my kids were 'getting in my way.'

I gratefully traded this particular disheartening method in for one of my new favorite features of Mind Organization, a "Next Actions" List. This particularly lovely and wonderfully handy piece of paper is created during my planning sessions each week. It is a way for me to take care of essentials while moving a few select projects forward simply. I love how the M.O.M. System helps me to organize my projects and tasks into "baby steps"— simple actions that go on my "important next actions" or "immediate next actions" lists.

I also love how the program has helped me to organize my "next actions" by context. I've got a "phone" list, an "errands" list, a "computer" list, a "do with the kids" list, etc., rather than a long, overwhelming list with no real flow to it. I also love the "someday" folder the program helped me create where I can write down and not lose track of all the great ideas and hopes I've got. I know I'll get to the many things on my "someday" list when the time is right—and I don't have to worry about forgetting them.

These new ways of thinking through and organizing my tasks have helped me to be more effective with my time. Now I know just what to do with a few spare minutes with energetic kids or a rare hour of uninterrupted quiet time. Rather than undertake to conquer a list from top to bottom, I can accomplish what I have time and energy for and what works best for my kids after referring to my nicely organized lists. And I enjoy it! I take pleasure in my daily tasks because planning my next actions has made it easy for me to stay motivated. The pending items on my now manageable "Next Actions" List can wait when dress ups and toe nail painting sometimes cannot.

Mind Organization for Moms has given me tools to see that an organized momma is a happy momma. I have learned the hard way that I can't do it all. (I also realize I don't want to do it all!) Instead I've learned to focus on determining what I can and should do now. I am discovering what things can wait. And I am learning how to keep tabs on those things I want to do, someday, that I don't have the time or energy for now. It is liberating and exhilarating. Some days my apartment is messier, some days my next-action list gets tossed to the side. And some weeks I tackle a long list of things that needed to be done. Thankfully I don't have to compromise my family's happiness to be productive. I don't have to live with a burden of "mom guilt." I feel confident that when I make efforts to keep my mind organized I am able to plan, prepare and organize. As a result I am learning to dream and enjoying the journey more than ever.

- Danielle Porter

Planning Sessions

No matter what system you choose to organize your projects and goals, it's vital to set up a regular time when you'll assess how your systems are working and plan for the upcoming week (this is called the "Weekly Review" in the M.O.M. program). I like to do it on Sunday nights. I spend about a half hour looking back over my past week, looking at the calendar, thinking through what tasks would need to be accomplished each day to make the calendar items work, and setting goals for the upcoming week. I use the Power of Moms Bloom Game to help me set goals—It makes it so easy to set balanced, bite-sized goals and I can print out a sheet where I track the accomplishment of my goals.

After I've worked on my own schedule and task lists for the week, I get together with my husband, and we spend a little time discussing the things we've got on our calendars for the week, what we need to do to support each other and the kids in the calendar items, and what our personal goals are for the week. We talk about any concerns we have about our family and/or individual kids and talk about longer-term goals and plans as well as immediate weekly needs.

Just as any effective company or organization has regular staff meetings, the management team of the family, you and your husband or partner (if you're blessed to have one), need a regular time to discuss what is coming up, what you're both working on and any concerns and ideas that have come up over the past week.

Time and Routine Organization

Effectively managing the timing of activities in our lives as moms is a vital part of organization. When we're saying "hurry, hurry, hurry!" to our children all the time, stress levels go way up for us and for our kids. When we can be realistic about how long things will take and pad our time estimates, we have a much better chance of being on time to things and feeling calm.

According to one mom:

> *Timing seems to be a major key for being organized. I've had so many moms say to me, "I just don't know how you do it with nine children." Right now, I'm still figuring it out myself! But I do know that once you have one child, you're a mom. And, with each child you add to your family, you're still a mom. Your timing is just different with two than with one. Part of timing everything right is knowing how much time it takes you to get a project done and then planning ahead to have time to accomplish it. For example, when my family goes anywhere, I*

> *aim to start loading kids into the car a half an hour before I*
> *need to arrive—plus driving time. That's the time it takes my*
> *family to get somewhere on time.*

-Sharla Olsen

Routines can really help us organize our time. And routines make kids feel safe.

Last year, we moved to a new city and a new house just before the holidays, which sent our family routines for a serious loop. We had some serious lateness issues, and that made for a frazzled mom and rushed, unhappy kids. After a particularly bad week, we sat down as a family and had a serious talk about our school-day routine. We identified some of the things that were making us late and we talked through all the specific things that need to happen to get out the door on time in the mornings. We came up with these basic daily standards:

- We lay out our school clothes the night before.
- We make beds when we stand up out of bed.
- We brush teeth when we go to the bathroom in the morning.
- We take a shower before we get dressed (we were having troubles with kids getting dressed then realizing they were supposed to take a shower and that was adding a lot of extra minutes . . .).
- We don't play or eat before we're dressed and ready.
- We put our socks on before we come downstairs so we don't have to go back upstairs and get them.
- We keep our shoes in the shoe place by the door.
- We meet at the breakfast table at 7:15.
- Mom doesn't look at email or answer phone calls before school.

The next morning went really well. I got all the big kids to school on time for the first time since the move. After dropping off the big kids, the twins and I had a quality reading time and I so enjoyed snuggling with them by the fire while we read. I replied to a handful of emails while they drew pictures (30 minutes of email time in the mornings—max—that was one of the boundaries I realized I needed to have), then we had a nice little lunch together before I took them to school (another routine standard—lunch at 11:15 so they can be at school by noon—and we were on time!). I came home, got dinner in the crock pot (another routine standard—figure out what to have for dinner at lunch time or before), and spent the time while the twins were at school really working through quite a bit of my "next actions" list for things I need to do when the kids aren't going to interrupt me. It was a great day!

Of course, most days the established routines get messed up here and there. Unexpected things pop up—usually at the least opportune times. The repairman shows up when you need to go pick up the kids from school. Someone calls with a crisis when you're trying to help your kids with homework and you probably shouldn't have answered the phone right then but you did (or one of your kids did). Your two-year-old twins dump out 20 pounds of pinto beans in the pantry while you're downstairs cleaning up the potted plant they upturned a few minutes prior while you were trying to do story time with your older kids. (This happened to me a few years ago. And similar sorts of things happened again and again almost every day while my twins were two. Any semblance of a routine was hard in those days—but still, days when I tried for a nice simple routine went better than those when I didn't even attempt a routine.)

Having a routine that generally works is a very good thing. Having times where you can usually plan on a little quiet time to get things done, time when you plan on helping with homework and time when you plan on running errands is a good thing. Being able to "blame" the clock for the necessity of doing certain things at certain times can be a great thing with kids—and can help you be more personally disciplined as well. Knowing what to expect and setting up expectations for your family members about how the day should go generally makes the day go better—as long as your expectations are realistic and you are ready to be flexible as needed, that is.

But please remember: Just as it's important to decide when and how to DO things, it's also important to decide when NOT to do things. You've heard the quote, "Never put off until tomorrow that which you can do today." Well, this saying is quite nice in some ways, but as any mother knows, there are tons of things that need to be put off or need to be added because of needs and moments that never could have been put on our calendar or list when we did our planning. My parents coined this new saying that I believe works much better: "ALWAYS put off a 'put-offable' in favor of a 'now or never.'" And I'll add: "Don't feel guilty about putting off something non-essential for something that really matters!"

Family Organization

As I was researching quotes about organization (I love a good quote), pretty much everything that came up was about organizations, not about being organized. At first I was annoyed. Then I started reading some of the quotes and started thinking about how we call groups of people working together towards a common mission an "organization" (whether they're actually organized or not) and how families are really organizations—organizations that need to be organized in similar ways to companies and non-profit organizations.

Just as great businesses, charities, and nations don't crop up of their own accord, strong families don't just happen. They are built with thought, love, planning, and yes, organization.

Having been raised by New York Times bestselling parenting authors, Richard and Linda Eyre, who focus on helping parents develop methods and systems for pro-active parenting, I have quite a bit to say on the subject of family organization. In fact, I have way more to say than can fit in this little essay. But I'll share some basic principles here and you can find a whole lot more at The Power of Moms if this whets your appetite.

I've found through my growing-up experiences, through my experiences building my own family with my husband, and through being a keen observer of families far and wide, that pro-active parenting is much more effective than reactive parenting. When you think about what you want your children to be gaining and then build methods and systems that support these purposes, beautiful things can happen (but sure, it can take a lot of patience and trial and error).

I suggest that you sit down with your husband and talk about what traits and abilities you want your kids to have when they "graduate" from your home and from your daily parenting at some point down the road. I'm guessing you'll come up with something like the list below:

- responsible with money
- empathetic towards others
- helpful
- polite
- kind
- excited about learning and growing and progressing
- able to clean and cook for themselves
- able to work hard and stick with a job
- able to set and accomplish goals
- skilled and talented in various areas
- firm in their understanding of who they are and what they stand for

Once you have your list, think through what methods and ideas you can use to help your children develop each of these skills and character traits. And then you'll want to set up regular "staff meetings" (including you, your spouse or parenting partner, and maybe some of your older children) for your "organization" (your family) so that you can discuss new programs, goals and methods and how things have progressed since the last meeting.

Organizing your family like an organization, with pro-active plans that lead to short and long-term goals, is a vital part of organization.

Chip Away

This essay just touches the tip of the organization iceberg. But hopefully it's helped you to think of a few specific areas where you may want to enhance your level of organization.

Organization is something you chip away at—focusing on one area at a time and regularly assessing and reassessing what you can do to better organize your things, your time, your thoughts and your progress towards what really matters to you and your family.

Here's one place to start: Take a few minutes to list all the areas of your life (and of your home) that need to be organized. You could make this list in the four categories this essay focuses on: Things, Thoughts, Time and Tasks, and Family Systems. Then, before you get overwhelmed by your list, circle the ONE thing in each category that is bothering you the most. Work on some methods for those things you've circled for a week or a month. Then move on to some other items on your list. Little by little, in an organized way, you'll feel more and more organized!

Of course, organizing will never be "done." As your family grows, your children get older, your projects and goals change, and your responsibilities are adjusted, your organizational methods and systems will have to change too. This is why those weekly "staff meetings" with those involved in your family organization and those weekly planning meetings with yourself are so important.

All of us will have different challenges and strengths when it comes to organization, but all of us can find great power as we chip away at developing practices and systems that help us feel more of the power of organization in our lives.

JOY

Tiffany Sowby's passionate dream from childhood—to grow up and be a mother—has come true, as she is now the mother of five children—three boys and two girls, ranging in age from 3 to 14. Though the realities of motherhood are often far from dreamy, Tiffany does her best to keep her passion for motherhood alive by appreciating, recognizing, and finding joy in the little things of life.

As a mom, Tiffany enjoys spontaneous thank-yous, children's laughter, laundry, hand-written notes and drawings, and nap time. Outside of motherhood, some of Tiffany's favorite things are date nights, writing, shoes, long conversations with friends, and rainy days.

While Tiffany's diploma from the University of Utah is filed away in a drawer somewhere, Tiffany has chosen to focus her time and efforts into motherhood. Through writing and speaking, Tiffany is committed to helping other mothers find contentment and joy in motherhood. Two of Tiffany's greatest passions, writing and motherhood, come together at ourmostofthetimehappyfamily.blogspot.com.

CHAPTER TEN

PUTTING EXTRA IN THE ORDINARY

The Power of Fun

by Tiffany Sowby

Recently, as lunchtime approached, my three-year-old son Joshua sat at the kitchen table saying, "I'm starving," while I ran around the kitchen unloading dishes, sorting papers, and dealing with phone calls. I was in a typical late morning routine and I needed a few more minutes to finish up a phone call and put away some dishes before making lunch. All Joshua wanted was some lunch, and maybe some attention. After getting off the phone and hearing a second declaration of starvation, I realized my tasks could wait. To my son's pleasant surprise, I stood in front of him at the kitchen table with a pen and paper in my hand and politely announced, "Welcome to Tiffany's Kitchen. What can I get for you to drink today?" I barely heard his words, "apple juice," because of the giggles that ensued. While the dishwasher sat open, my three-year-old and I played restaurant. I don't know if I've *ever* seen Joshua smile that big while eating lunch.

As mothers, we have demands on us all day every day. Even nighttime hours are not exempt from the duties of motherhood. Middle-of-the-night feedings, sick children, and bad dreams muddle together with the daytime tasks of laundry, house cleaning, employment, volunteer work, and meal preparation that require practically all of our time, effort, and energy. How can we make sure that neither our families nor we are dragged down with the myriad of tasks that could very easily overwhelm all of our days? It starts by simply reminding ourselves that there is more to life than laundry.

Most of us as very young mothers, and of course as pre-mothers, planned on being *fun* mothers. We envisioned story times, play times, creative projects, and traditions that we believed—no matter what—we *would* do. And then something happened. We became mothers! Before we knew it, our time was filled with responsibilities: bills to pay, housework to do, faces to wipe, stains to launder, and so much more. Whatever happened to those early visions of homemade piñatas, beautifully-decorated cookies for every holiday, picnic lunches on the family room floor, and nature walks?

> *"People rarely succeed unless they have fun in what they are doing."*
> - Dale Carnegie

Every mother wants to be successful. Every family wants to succeed. Have you ever thought "fun" might be the missing ingredient you need to get to the success you want? Do you ever find yourself rushing through your days acting as though fun is to be reserved for a time when, and only when, you have completed all other tasks, chores, and responsibilities on that never-ending "to-do-list"?

The reality is that putting a little more fun in our personal and family life can potentially make us *more* successful, not less—not to mention much happier throughout the journey. When we make the effort to team up fun and responsibility, we'll begin to see for ourselves that fun is actually a vital part of success.

Opportunities to incorporate fun into our lives are all around us. Sometimes we just have to slow down so we don't miss them.

Sometimes, we need to forget about the "to-do-list" and just let it happen. While the definition of fun will vary for individuals and families (based on circumstances and interests), the need to have fun within a family remains universal. So how do you start having more fun? The following sections illustrate four aspects of fun that can easily be incorporated into family life: family traditions, simple times, spontaneous moments, and putting *extra* in the ordinary.

Family Traditions

Every family has traditions. Some are deliberate celebrations of milestones and holidays such as a first birthday or the first day of school. Others are less intentional, developing out of weekly rituals such as Saturday chores or Friday night pizza. Some traditions are short-lived, while others are treasured practices that are passed down through generations. Traditions are found in every family, making them an ideal avenue for incorporating FUN into family life.

One of our family's favorite traditions is celebrating "half birthdays." We keep it simple: an inexpensive gift, *half* a chocolate cake (with *half* a candle in it), and the first *half* of the traditional "Happy Birthday" song sung. Just after my son recently blew out the broken-in-half candle atop his half cake, my daughter said to me, "Half birthdays are fun. Everyone celebrates birthdays, but not everyone does half birthdays. They're *fun*." Sometimes it is the small, simple traditions that bring fun into our routine lives.

An advantage of this tradition is that it has a "set date." The half-birthday date finds a presence on the family calendar and inserts fun when it would otherwise be filled with normal routines and tasks.

With a little effort, even the more serious and "necessary" traditions or routines can become more pleasurable. Each Sunday, as a family, we hold a Family Council. It is a rather somber meeting when we discuss and journal the past week's events, and then give each child the opportunity to bring up any "matters of importance." Last year, my daughter Megan was acting as the scribe recording the meeting in our Family Council Book. As she flipped through the book looking for the next clean page, she started to laugh. She paused and read about a Family Council from almost seven years ago. As a family we laughed aloud as she read her "matter of importance": "Keep my new pajamas clean so I can wear them every night." What was once a "matter of importance" to her as a five-year-old girl now seemed silly and trivial. It was funny! Our Family Council agenda now includes reading an entry from a previous Family Council. Without fail, we laugh every time. What could be a dry and boring family meeting has become *fun*!

Another of our family traditions falls on March 2nd. As an adult, the day always stood out in my mind because of a silly memory from back in my college days. Later, when I had three young children, my grandfather passed away on this day. A couple of years after he died, I thought about the reasons that particular day stood out in my mind. Throw into the mix that it is Dr. Seuss' birthday, and I had all the motivation I needed to start a new family tradition! Our celebration is very simple. Upon waking up, my children find a new Dr. Seuss book on the kitchen table. At dinner, we tell a story about my grandpa and I regale them with the silly memory from college. It isn't a big event, but it's enough for good memories. Take it from my daughter Ellie, who recently asked, "When's that day we get a new book on the table? That's a fun day."

Traditions will naturally vary from family to family. When selecting traditions for your family, pay attention to what your family considers fun. Ultimately, the most important part of the tradition is spending quality time together.

This mom points out some important considerations when selecting family traditions:

Pick traditions that suit your family. If your husband or kids can't stay on pitch, then caroling at retirement homes may not be your best option.

My way isn't the only way. When deciding which traditions you'd like your family to have, it's easy to think the way your family did things when you were growing up is the best and only way to do it. If you let yourself believe this fallacy, your family will miss out on some wonderful memories.

When I was growing up, Christmas Eve meant gathering with our cousins to reenact the Nativity in full costume, complete with musical numbers. My husband's extended family also gathered on Christmas Eve, but to play ball. Everybody went down to the college court to play basketball in the big family tournament.

It was easy for me to think that performing the Nativity is the ideal way to unite a family in love and purpose. But imagine a family of athletic boys being forced by their mother to "wear that bathrobe and aluminum foil crown, and do it with a smile!" That doesn't exactly engender feelings of warmth and family unity. My husband's tradition of a basketball game is something they have really loved. It has tied them together, just as my family's tradition tied us closer every year.

Life is short; enjoy it to the fullest. Fill your family life with fun by making traditions that bind you to those you love.

- Heather Whitehead

Another adds this important thought:

Traditions are for the whole family. My grandmother, Iva Lou Herd, was a huge proponent of having the adults and the children play together. Every September we had a family reunion *at a lake. It was a cardinal rule that EVERYONE participated in the official Herd Family Reunion Field Games and Treasure Hunt. As always, my grandmother's methods proved to be right. It was so fun watching uncles and cousins, with giggling toddlers clinging to their backs, running from clue to clue. When someone tripped and fell, there was always someone bigger to scoop them up and encourage them to keep laughing (and quit crying). And there was no greater excitement than when, amidst the three-legged race, one of the big, strong uncles went crashing down making way for two little nephews to bound their way across the finish line to glory—now that was a victory! There was always lots of cheering and laughter . . . as they say, the more the merrier. These events became the highlight of our reunions, and the real treasure was everyone having fun <u>together</u>.*

- Shawnie Sutorius

Whether you are looking for new traditions or evaluating those you currently have, take a moment to consider if having fun is a part of them. Incorporating fun into traditions will make them more appealing to everyone.

Simple Times

Too often, we have the tendency to over-complicate and over-plan activities, yet it's the little things that children tend to notice and remember. What mother hasn't had a child more interested in the wrapping paper or cardboard box than the item inside? While an activity may not always go as we originally planned, by keeping our traditions and activities simple, often the end result works just as well. (If not better!)

Last summer, I asked my children what they remembered as being the most fun from the previous summer. The replies included: "The time we went on a picnic and I caught fish in the plastic container the treats had been in," "Pretending we were camping in the back yard," "Dad re-arranging rocks and making a pretend hot tub in the canyon creek." Do you see a pattern here? None of my children mentioned a visit to an amusement park, the local swimming pool, or a vacation. While those outings certainly have a place in family memories and activities, sometimes it is the simple, creative events that really stand out to our kids. (And are often far less stress and preparation than field trips and vacations!)

Here's an example of a simple, creative game:

> *A game we love to play is the Paper Bag Game. You divide into two teams and everyone gets their own brown lunch sack with something in it that they have to eat. We vary the food to add a little excitement because you never know what you are going to get in your bag—delicious or detestable! After everyone is standing in front of a bag you start with the person at the head of the table. As soon as the first person has finished their food the next person can go and so on and so forth. The first team to go through everyone wins! If you do not have enough people to make teams, just put a timer on and try to do it under a certain amount of time. This is great for a family night or when the kids have some friends over to play. You can use anything you have in your cupboards—just make sure no one peeks in their bag before it is their turn!*
>
> *I want you to know that my children do not readily shout with joy at my ideas. They most always think they will be "dumb and boring." But once I get them to actually do it, (I totally ignore their whining) they love it.*
>
> *- Allyson Smith*

A couple of Halloweens ago, my kids asked to go to our local recreation center for a Halloween carnival. Having been a couple of years earlier, I was not keen on repeating the event with five children (including a baby who was six months old). I didn't want to disappoint my children, so I racked my brain for a replacement activity. That first 'Family Carnefel' (as the homemade sign of our then seven-year-old stated) was the beginning of an affordable, simple and fun family event that we continue to enjoy. On a random weekend, when we have a free night and some creative energy, each family member is placed in charge of an event. We've had activities as simple as tossing a coin into a bowl, as well as more challenging cowboy roping contests. We've tried balloon trains around the house, eating donuts from a string, and passing cereal from straw to straw. A Family—or neighborhood—Carnefel is guaranteed to elicit plenty of laughter.

I am a believer that in doing simple things together, some of the best relationships can blossom. Simple activities are easy to fit into hectic schedules and require little planning. This mom clearly understands this:

> *Not long ago I taught my girls how to play Rummy and Nertz.*
> *Now, there is nothing they would rather do with me. Marissa,*
> *in particular, often talks me into "just one game" before bed. It*
> *only takes a few minutes, costs nothing, and always has us*
> *laughing and interacting. Elaborate and expensive activities,*
> *while wonderful to do once in a while, tend to be overwhelming*
> *or impractical to do very often.*
>
> *- Shawnie Sutorius*

Really, it isn't hard to have fun with our children. The little impromptu restaurant episode with my son that busy lunchtime entertained him every bit as much as an outing to a fast-food eatery's play zone would have.

"At the end of your life, you will never regret not having passed one more test, not winning one more verdict or not closing one more deal. You will regret time not spent with a husband, a friend, a child, or a parent."
-Barbara Bush

Time spent with our families doesn't have to be anything grand. It is quite often in the most simple, unplanned moments we make some of our best memories!

Spontaneous Moments

Oftentimes we underestimate the ease with which we can incorporate fun and laughter into our family's lives. Sure there may be extra clean up and work later, but first there is the fun, and that is the part that everyone will remember.

One mom shares this experience (and I would like to think I would enjoy the humor, spontaneity and FUN in this experience had it happened to me . . .).

> *I will never forget the hot summer afternoon that my father hid in the bushes for nearly thirty minutes, garden hose in hand, waiting for my mother to arrive home from the store and walk into the house. As her car pulled into the drive, my heart began to race as I heard my father stifle a childlike giggle. As soon as she was within range, he roared from the bushes soaking her from head to toe! Soon, he turned on the children. Within moments, we all stood on the lawn, wet with water and tears of laughter.*

> *Then, the challenge was issued. Someone had to get back at Dad!*

> *It was a few weeks later when I saw my Mom dragging the garden hose inside the house. We followed her, curious as to what she could possibly be doing. She held her finger to her lips, begging our silence; she then tiptoed into the bathroom, hose in*

hand, where my father was taking a nice, warm shower. Oh, how he yelped when that icy water hit his shoulders! I don't think I've ever heard my mother laugh so hard. Looking back, I realize how important it was for me, as a child, to see my parents having fun. Laughter makes us feel secure. It relieves tension. It relaxes our minds. It brings families closer. Nothing warms my heart quite as much as the sound of their sincere, unabashed laughter.

- Jenny Proctor

A few months ago, I heeded a challenge to add more "serendipitous moments" into my mothering. It seemed almost providential that just days after committing to the challenge, I drove past a local park, with all of my children in tow. My six-year-old asked if we could stop and play. I'm not quite sure who was more surprised, me or the children, when I turned into the parking lot in spite of the fact dinner needed to be on the table in thirty minutes. The kids had fun playing at the park while my eldest child and I sat alone in the car talking. As I called out to the children that it was time to go, I silently praised myself for giving into the moment. The pleasant visit to the park came to a screeching halt when my six-year-old had a temper tantrum about leaving and my eight-year-old attempted to rein her into the car with his cowboy roping rope. Though it temporarily left me second-guessing my efforts to be a 'fun mom', months later, we all laugh about the spontaneous trip to the park.

Life can get crazy and hectic for all of us. There are deadlines, tests, appointments, schedules, and outings that must be managed. But amidst these daily pressures, we cannot forget to have fun.

Sometimes every day seems exactly the same as the day before. I get so wrapped up in the routine motherly duties that each day blurs into the next, and before I know it another week has gone by! I find myself struggling to remember what we did in any given week, or what I even accomplished. I need to slow down and remember that when I'm a cute little old lady (as opposed to an ugly old lady), it's not going to be the household duties and chores that I remember, it's going to be the games, the laughter and the FUN that I had with my children. That being said, these memories aren't going to create themselves; I need to put down the dish rag and the soap to have some spontaneous fun with my kids!

- Shayne Dickson

Surely you can all relate to the following scene: Mom's trying to cook dinner, homework is being done at the kitchen table, a child is typing a report at the computer, a toddler is underfoot, the phone is ringing, neighbor kids are knocking at the door looking for a playmate and somebody needs a Band-Aid RIGHT NOW. What do you do? The most tempting solution for me is often to run away from it all, but of course that wouldn't help anything. Very often during these chaotic moments, I turn the nearby radio on. I grab a makeshift microphone (usually a utensil, pencil, or broom) and begin singing loudly. Sometimes I'll even hop up on a nearby chair. This spontaneous outburst works like magic (almost) every time. Somehow, even with loud music and several voices singing, the chaos dissipates, the tension disappears, and by the time the song ends everybody is rejuvenated and ready to continue with their tasks.

Consider this experience that required no clean-up and no preparation—just a little imagination (and spontaneity):

> *One afternoon I was relishing the fact that my boys were contently playing. It was a great opportunity to get some writing done.*
>
> *As I listened to their distant laughter, I felt a little prompting to join them. Moments like these don't come along very often, one*

part of me reasoned. The kids are happily playing and I can get some writing done, the other part of me said. But, then I heard it in a different way: Moments like these don't come along very often, when the kids are happily playing and I can spontaneously join in on the fun.

Joining them won out.

I poked my head into the room and saw they were playing Pokemon. I jumped into the room and onto the bed shouting 'lightning strike!' with my arms shooting out lightning bolts. The look of surprise on my children's faces was priceless. For the next twenty minutes or so we laughed and played, and I received hug after hug from my boys. They seemed overjoyed I had joined in with such enthusiasm. This was a moment, purely spontaneous, which I seized instead of letting it slip by. It didn't require a lot of time or effort, but I am grateful I followed the prompting because we shared a priceless moment none of us will forget.

- Chantelle Adams

Motherhood is certainly not easy. Duty calls often, and it is all too easy to get caught up in the day-to-day responsibilities that demand our attention. Try looking at it a little differently though: Since our duties are demanding, we certainly aren't going to forget about them; so why don't we occasionally pause and have some fun? Nothing that is really important will get left undone just because we have stopped to enjoy a funny moment. In fact, sometimes the funny moment may be the very thing we need to get our work done, as this mom can attest:

I had promised to make some lemon bars for a baby shower one day. I was naturally crunched for time. My kids were at my feet begging me to let them up on the counter to help. Seriously, if I did not let them up on the counter they were going to DIE! They needed to help me THAT BAD! I was starting to get flustered and wanted them out of my way, preferably someplace far like Australia.

This was one of those moments when I knew my attitude would either make or break the household mood for the rest of the day. I had some choices to make. One: Go to my happy place and pretend that my children really are in Australia, and then maybe I won't notice the annoying pleading. Two: Give in, let them help, and hope no one notices some mystery ingredients in the lemon bars. Three: Bring out the spontaneous kid buried inside of me and make this a game. Everyone loves games, right?

I had some leftover lemon juice. (We all know where this is going . . .) I told my kids that I needed some taste testers to see if my "lemonade" was still fresh. Giddy with anticipation I had my video camera ready. Let the taste testing begin!

My oldest, Remi, took one sip and knew what I was up to. Corr, my youngest, not so much. He chugged the entire thing! He put down the glass and got a bad case of the sour shivers, or to be more accurate, sour convulsions. We were hysterical, despite the sour lemon juice, and best of all made an awesome video! My kids kept themselves busy watching the video over and over, while I finished my lemon bars in peace. Instead of it being just another boring day in the kitchen, we will always remember it as the fun lemon juice day—even if my kids are terrified of lemonade for the rest of their lives!

- Shayne Dickson

We have to remember that spontaneity requires choice. These sorts of memories can only be made if we value having fun with our family enough to give into the moment.

Putting Extra in Ordinary Days

Early in my mothering career, I sat in a meeting about family activity ideas. The lady presenting the lecture told of a time her school-age daughter didn't want to go to a friend's house after school, as she worried about what fun she may miss out on at home. That thought profoundly affected me, and made me ask myself, "What can I do so my children think of our home as a fun place and believe that every day is not just going to be an ordinary day?"

Now, I have to admit, the majority of days in our house *are ordinary days* and I absolutely love and treasure them. The sounds of an instrument being practiced, a dryer running, and a toddler pushing a toy car along the kitchen floor make for a pleasant soundtrack to a lovely, ordinary day. But, who doesn't like to have something thrown in to inject a little fun into our otherwise-routine days? It is often the pleasantly ordinary days that make the perfect backdrop for a splash of fun.

> *There are always jobs to be done, so why not include your children and make it fun? I have turned dusting into a scavenger hunt. We always turn the music up so we can dance and sing while we work. My kids love to help in the garden because we dig holes, find bugs, watch things miraculously grow, and then eat the fruits of their labors. It sometimes takes a bit longer to complete the tasks, but this kind of "fun" allows you to teach the importance of work and responsibility to your children while spending quality time together.*
>
> *- Chantelle Adams*

One of my children's favorite things to do, that adds a little "extra" to the ordinary, is an after-school treasure hunt. There is no set schedule to when I may do one. (Honestly it depends on my schedule and energy.) There is sheer delight on my children's faces when they enter the kitchen after a long day at school to find the tell-tale signs of a treasure hunt on the pantry door. It usually starts with a drawing or rhyme that tells them where to go next. The four to five scattered clues that follow take them upstairs, downstairs and even outside. I love to watch the teamwork and giggles that ensue as a result of my inept drawings or silly throw-words-together-because-they-rhyme type clues. (Do not let me fool you. We have plenty of "Stop, you're going too fast," or "You lied, you said I could read the next one.")

Though the "treasure" at the end is rarely anything more than a simple after-school snack, really, who wouldn't laugh to find a plate of cookies sitting in an empty bathtub? Even my teenager follows along happily (albeit with a tad less enthusiasm than the others). After all, who really ever outgrows fun?

Even our smallest attempts to add a little extra to the ordinary will be recognized and appreciated by our children. March 2nd is an ordinary day for most people. It used to be ordinary for us, until I threw in a little extra. Setting a new book on the kitchen table and retelling stories are nothing special, but they are just slightly out of the ordinary, and that's enough to make the day fun. Pick a day, just any old day, and put a little extra into it. You'll be amazed at the little jumpstart and renewal it will give to everyone involved.

It isn't just our own families who may benefit from our efforts. Sometimes other mothers may be touched by the power of our example. One mom shares the following charming account of such a time:

> *Splash, Splash, Splash! I could see a mother splashing in the puddles from last night's rainstorm with her children. Two girls, pigtails bobbing, held hands as they jumped in puddles of warm rainwater. A boy, pedaling with all his might, was racing his*

bike through the largest puddle. Another daughter was leaping across small puddles.

Puddle-jumping is just one of the many simple and fun ways this mother, my neighbor, spends time with her children. It seems she is always adding fun into their days. Once after dropping something off at my house, I noticed her stop for a few minutes at the park with her son. They slid down the slide a few times, and then continued home. Just a simple action, but fun for a child. She draws with sidewalk chalk, paints with watercolors, dribbles a soccer ball and builds snow forts. I've seen her at the park tossing a baseball with her husband while their children play.

When I first met her, I thought she was an ordinary mother. After watching for years, I recognized that she is an extraordinary mother. Her children, who are becoming teenagers, are good-natured. They make good choices and have an unusually calm and relaxed relationship with their mother.

This mother has become a role model for me. She keeps her life simplified (even with five children) and minimizes the clutter around her house. Those two habits enable a few minutes of unrushed time nearly every day. Mothering is one of her priorities, and she consistently chooses to use her few daily minutes for her children. She makes life happy for them. Not just for them, but with them.

Following her model of creating simple, fun times has required me to work hard, especially at first. I needed to minimize distractions and clutter. Then I needed to prioritize "fun" every day, with every child. Initially I had to plan the time (ten or fifteen minutes every day) and the activity (such as reading stories, singing songs, or playing with play-dough). After a lot of conscious effort, simple fun is becoming a natural part of my mothering. Choosing to create a fun and happy climate has increased happy laughter and family closeness.

This mother I admire once told me, "Someday when I am old, and it is raining, I hope my children will call me up and say, 'Do you remember when you used to take us puddle jumping?' and I'll smile and remember."

- Allyson Smith

Embrace the Fun

Jump in a few puddles, put the after-school snack in the empty bathtub, or slide down a slide before you leave the park. It doesn't take much to put a little "extra" in an ordinary day.

Remember how you once envisioned motherhood? We needn't feel encumbered by the grandiose plans of yesteryear. We need to look at the mothers we are now. By putting some thought and effort into our family traditions, keeping things simple, being willing to seize spontaneous moments, and adding some extra to the ordinary, we *can* be the fun mothers we hoped to be.

There is room for fun! There is more to life than laundry! Whether it is a family vacation, a last-minute picnic, or a case of the giggles at bedtime, we all need a momentary escape from the responsibilities and seriousness of life. Our children, and even we, will benefit from the results of incorporating fun, laughter, and humor into our lives. Fun is all around us, we may just have to look harder some days than others to find it.

April is a Co-Founder of The Power of Moms and is native to Long Beach, California—where she grew up boogie boarding with her dad and doing aerobic exercises up and down the hallway with her mom to "Mony Mony." She developed a love for writing at the age of six and went on to major in communication studies with a minor in family science.

Throughout her college parenting classes, she was sure that she was going to be a fun mom—enjoying hay rides, a daily batch of brownies, and science lessons around the kitchen table. The first 12 years of motherhood, however, pretty much put her into survival mode. But now that her children, Alia, Grace, Ethan, and Spencer, sleep through the night and put on their own shoes (yay!), she's starting to rediscover the "fun."

April and her husband/soul-mate, Eric, live in Southern California, where they do their best to build a strong family and be as helpful as possible to others wanting to do the same. You can find their family blog at powerofafamily.blogspot.com.

CHAPTER ELEVEN

SOMEDAY I'LL SHOWER BEFORE NOON

The Power of Optimism

by April Perry

Here are some details captured at the end of a particularly frustrating day when my children were small:

No shower. Never left the house. One child pounded through piano practice . . .just to prove a point. Tried to do a 20-minute exercise video, but all the children wanted to do it with me in a tiny area of our living room, and then they started being silly and jumping on my back, so I sent them to their rooms. I ambitiously tried to bake bread, which got ruined because the oven control locks don't work when the oven is on. Children wanted to eat every 20 minutes the entire day (why did I let them?). A couple of stressful family issues needed to be handled. Forgot to grease the pizza pan, so we had to pry our dinner off. Spilled smoothie on freshly-washed pants. Tried to get work done during the first half of naptime, toddler woke up an hour early, so I never got to catch up on sleep. Three-year-old screamed at LEAST 50 times throughout the morning. Five loads of laundry. Dusty house.

Am I supposed to be optimistic during days like this? I realize that I'm lucky to have a house, a healthy body, food to eat and children to love, but is it totally unrealistic to want a shower in the morning, a few minutes to exercise, and some sense of order?

When I'm feeling discouraged, grumpy or impatient, the *last* thing I want to hear is that I should "look on the bright side," "change my attitude," or "count my blessings." Typically, I want to feel understood. I want to know that it's normal for me to be struggling. Well, I've discovered that it *is* normal, but I've also learned that there is incredible power in learning to be optimistic.

Let's Define Optimism

I know this is a basic word, but I was confused for a long time. I thought optimism meant I was supposed to *love* messy diapers. I thought mothers naturally danced around the kitchen and opened their arms lovingly when their children woke up at 2 a.m. The ideal mother would smile 24/7, would be described as "peppy" and "giddy," and would never—ever—hide in the closet to cry.

The *actual* definition of optimism is "the tendency to expect the best and see the best in all things" (Webster's online dictionary). Of *course* you're not supposed to love the mess and stress and worries of motherhood; it's the results you love: the daughter who hugs you every six minutes, the son who leans *way* over the seat to kiss you before jumping out of the car at school, and the toddler who excitedly opens his arms and announces, "Right here, mom! I'm right here!" when he wakes up in the morning.

Here's one wise mom's perspective:

> *Being positive and optimistic doesn't mean I naively pretend there is no negative; being positive means I actively determine my focus and give energy to what aids me in learning and*

216

growth. There is no positive without negative. It's against the law; the natural law that is! It's like trying to separate two sides of a coin, or setting a cause in motion while hoping to avoid the effect. I think when we only desire positive and no negative at any given moment in our lives, we limit ourselves significantly. And in doing so, consider how much growth one might be missing. I admit it's easier said than done, but if I wanted easy I never would have chosen motherhood!

- Amy Oliver

Learning to grow through life's challenges while keeping a positive focus is a *skill*—one that anyone can develop. I've seen this modeled in the very worst of circumstances, and once I learned to apply it to *my* life, *everything* changed.

Here are some practical ideas that lift and inspire me on the days life seems too hard (if today is one of those days for you, I'm so sorry. You *will* get through this.)

Optimism Requires Action

For mothers everywhere, "life" comes fast—constantly trying to pull us down. We typically don't value the sandwiches we make or the lullabies we sing; instead, we're quick to notice how we "lost it" when our daughters were squabbling or our sons were playing Tarzan on the basketball hoop with their jump ropes. We also don't specifically spell out what we need in order to feel happy—we just get grumpy and expect our families to read our minds (or is that just me?). At the same time, we're being watched every minute. We're leaders facing constant pressure and heavy responsibilities.

So what are we going to *do* about this?

Optimism doesn't mean we shrug our shoulders at our failing circumstances or bad habits. Eating donuts and ice cream all day won't create "abs of steel"—no matter how many happy thoughts we send toward our midsections. We need to take action. When I (1) carefully examine my life, (2) identify what's *really* wrong, (3) make a specific plan to improve it, and (4) think optimistically as I follow my plan, *that* is when I feel like dancing in the kitchen. Working *toward* our goals brings just as much satisfaction as *achieving* them. It's sometimes painful, and it requires hard work, but action enables optimism.

I recently started experiencing some heavy anxiety, to the point where I was waking up at night feeling sick to my stomach. As much as I told myself to relax, I couldn't shake the stress. My pre-teen daughters would come to me, wanting to talk late into the night about the discussions on the lunch benches, the photography class they wanted to take, and their birthday party plans, and all I could manage was five minutes of chit-chat before sending them to bed—and then I'd spend the rest of the evening wondering what was wrong with me.

At that point, I knew I needed to change my course. Over the next few days, I invested several hours thinking, reading, brainstorming and praying. I realized that I'd over-scheduled my life, I'd let too much clutter creep into the house, I had pages and pages of ideas and tasks I hadn't processed, I had been eating too many cookies, I hadn't been taking time to *enjoy* my life and I wasn't spending my time on the most essential things.

Then I made a plan. I bought three excellent books on the subjects where I was weak (one about work/life management, one about healthy eating, and one about house cleaning), I quickly read through them and then I started applying the ideas I'd learned. Within *hours*, I started feeling optimistic. The clutter didn't go away all at once, but I knew I could get it under control within the month. I started thinking more about health, and the cookies didn't appeal to me as much. I stopped checking email every hour and established better boundaries with my computer work. Those simple changes, among others, helped me feel optimistic about creating my best life. It took a lot of work, but now I can sleep at night, and I feel happier when I'm with my family. It's worth the effort.

Find the "Something Beautiful" in Every Day

Having a family is a privilege. Even when things look like they can't get any worse, there's always *something* to smile about.

> *I could hear my seventeen-month-old son, Asher, in the kitchen, but I didn't have the strength to find out what he was up to. Five months pregnant, I had come down with a bad case of the stomach flu just the day before. I was relieved when I learned that the abdominal pain, constant body aches, fever, nausea and vomiting posed no danger to my baby; all I had to do was rest, stay hydrated and endure the symptoms. That much I could handle, but how was I supposed to take care of our home, my husband, my infinite to-do list and my adventurous son in the meantime?*

> *As I lay on the bed, just wishing this would all pass quickly so I could get on with my life, I heard a rustling close by. I opened my eyes and saw Asher come into the room with a bag of corn flakes. Apparently, our little one had pulled himself onto a chair and then onto the dining table, where he retrieved the cereal bag that my husband had opened earlier that day for breakfast. He proudly mounted onto the mattress where I was resting, and before I could stop him, turned the bag completely upside down! Corn flakes were everywhere—on the pillow, on the mattress, on the floor, and even in my hair and clothes. I could hear myself screaming in my mind, "Nooooo! Do~n't!" but I was too weak to mutter a word. I just lay there in disbelief.*

Naturally, Asher was thrilled with what he had just done. He bounced on his knees and giggled with excitement. I kept thinking, "I can't believe he just did this. What a mess! How am I going to clean this up?" But then I watched my son delicately pinch a corn flake between his tiny thumb and forefinger, slowly lean his body forward and push the corn flake onto my lips. He opened his mouth as if to say, "eat it"—and that's when I realized he wanted to feed me.

My heart filled with love, and I felt like we were both beaming. I could sense how pleased he was to be taking care of me, and I instantly felt so grateful for my son, my husband (who later cleaned up all the corn flakes), my pregnancy, our home, my health and so many other things in my life that I'm sure I wouldn't have thought of had this happened at any other time. The sickness was not at all pleasant, but this experience taught me to "watch," slow down and be grateful, for there is joy and love that can be found even in the midst of what seems like a huge mess.

- Becky Nibley Budge

We can all relate, can't we? When I think back to my most painful moments (miscarriages, surgeries, years without sleeping through the night, and personal struggles that led me to tears and to my knees) every single heartache is coupled with a sweet image I wouldn't trade for the world: "Get well" cards scrawled in crayon, a five-year-old vacuuming without being asked, a six-year-old changing his brother's diaper so his mom could sleep a little longer, or strawberry-scented foot massages and sliced cucumbers—picked from a salad in the fridge and placed on my eyes.

Sweetness surrounds us at every turn, and motherhood is an incredible opportunity! The secret is learning to see the beauty.

Awhile back, I was at my friend Cara's house. I was there to borrow some cute bud vases. I knew she would have a good selection, and she didn't disappoint.

Everywhere I turned in her house I saw something cute. Cute pillows. Cute drapes. Cute dishes. Cute frames. Cute, cute, cute!

I thought to myself, "If my house was this cute, I would be smiling all day long!" Which led to remembering something I had heard on a talk show. They say you should surround yourself with the things you love.

On my way home I was worried. My house is always under construction. I had a concrete floor at the time. My dishes don't match. My walls are bare. You get the idea. How could I be happy if I'm not surrounded by things that I love?

As soon as I asked that question, the answer came into my mind. Of course! I <u>am</u> surrounded by the things that I love—my wonderful children and husband.

I am definitely surrounded. Matching dishes can wait

- Christi Alston Davis

You *Choose* Optimism

One thing that helps me handle the discrepancy between the mom I *thought* I'd be and the mom I *am* is to say, "I choose to be happy."

When I'm cleaning up "potty accidents," juggling coloring books and crayons in cramped doctors' offices, or dealing with daughters who are as emotional as I am, I repeat over and over in my head, "I choose to be happy." Life is full of reasons to look on the bright side:

Like the majority of moms, I do the same repetitive jobs each day, seven days a week: sweep the floor, do laundry, fold and hang clothes, dust furniture, prepare meals, clean up those meals, mop the floor, vacuum here, vacuum there, wash more dishes, and somehow in between it all, manage to change a few hundred diapers. What I do feels like my own version of a movie called "Motherhood Groundhog Day," only my costume is gray sweats and my make-up is, well, none.

A few years ago I started to believe I had the most brainless, unappreciated, and certainly, most unglamorous job in the universe. I was doing my ten-thousandth load of laundry, robotically placing each piece of dirty underwear in the washing machine. I'd done this job so many times before that it certainly required no thinking and especially none of my hard-earned college degree. After loading all the clothes, I suddenly snapped out of my mechanical state and thought, "This is so mundane, this is so boring. I'm so tired of boring. I want engaging. I want pink stilettos, not sweats. I want intellectually stimulating! I want pizzazz! I want a change of scenery. I want out!"

And so I headed to Wal-Mart. (Believe me when I say that in my small town, this is often as electrifying and engaging as it gets!) As I threw this and that in my cart, I headed over to the scrapbook aisle. Now don't think for a second that one of my Super Mom qualities is scrap-booking, because to this day, it's not. But I'd considered taking up the hobby, so I went to this particular section of the store to see what I was up against.

As I browsed through the different sheets of scrapbook stickers, one in particular jumped out at me. There, typed in cute, squishy blue print was a phrase that grabbed my attention in a most life-changing way: "Always thank God for a normal, boring day."

There, of all places, was the answer. I had been looking at my day-to-day mundane tasks as a burden rather than a blessing. Instead of robotically doing laundry, I needed to be grateful I had all those cute little clothes to fold because it meant that after heart-wrenching infertility struggles, I was blessed to finally bear children. Instead of begrudgingly sweeping and mopping the kitchen floor, I needed to feel lucky that each member of my family was healthy enough to walk across the floor, even if they did have gobs of mud on their shoes.

In sum, what I often classified as a boring or monotonous day meant I hadn't taken any trips to the ER, my house didn't catch on fire, I never received a dreaded phone call with tragic news, my basement didn't flood and my husband arrived home safely from work. Standing in that store aisle, I thought of all the worst-case scenarios that could have gone wrong to break up the dullness of my daily, repetitive household tasks, making me feel grateful for all those typical, ho-hum days of motherhood.

- Jamie Jones Hadfield

There are lots of ways to bring fun, purpose and nobility into the monotony of family work, but really, the "boring" days are a blessing. We get to choose our perspective, and sometimes that simply means clarifying our focus:

After losing my second child during pregnancy, I realized how fragile this maternal journey I was on could be. During the long, hard days that followed my loss, I made a choice that I would focus on the things that brought happiness into my life. It was a deliberate, conscious choice and it really changed who I was as a mother.

I once heard an anecdote relating to this: look around the room and count as many blue things as you can. Then, close your eyes and list the yellow things you saw. Most people can't do this because they were too focused on the blue things.

I find the meaning of this so applicable to motherhood and all that it entails. If we only focus on the blue things, the hard things, the things we cannot control, the exhausting things, we can become completely blind to the yellow things, the beautiful, wonderful parts of motherhood that completely surround us.

We can choose which color we focus on, even though both colors are present in our lives.

On days when I am pushed to my limit, I remind myself of the gift that is motherhood and how grateful I am for it. I remind myself that while there are plenty of crazy days, there is nowhere else I would rather be than right here in the "thick of things" with my children.

- Felicity Aston

Beautifully said, don't you think?

Tell the Best Stories from Your Day

One day as a new mom, I videotaped my toddler screaming in her crib when she refused to take a nap. When my husband got home, I played the video so he could see what I had to "put up with." He lovingly said, "Honey, I'm sorry you had a rough day, but I don't videotape the worst parts of *my* day and show them to *you*."

That wasn't quite the response I'd expected, but you know what? He was right. I decided from that day forward to tell him the best stories from my day (and occasionally review and/or cry about the hard parts). I started keeping an eye out for the sweet, funny, clever moments that my husband missed.

"Today Alia and Ethan were singing songs and reading stories in the downstairs bathroom for a *really* long time. Finally they emerged, and Alia said, 'Ethan set a family record for sitting in the bathroom cupboard for 12 minutes.' I looked at Ethan, who had a huge smile plastered across his face as he reflected on his success. 'A family record!'"

Sometimes I tell how the children decorated the walls of the garage with coloring pages or how they made snack trays that looked like faces. I tell him how the baby can say a whole prayer by himself, and I show him the display of notes reading, "I love Mom." Sometimes I wonder if I'm falsely representing my reality, but I've noticed when I focus on the best stories of the day, those are the only parts I remember.

This process works for athletes, too (though I am not one). My brother-in-law Jim has played for and coached many athletic teams, and he said that sometimes coaches will only focus on the good—as a way to keep the players mentally strong and focused. Other times, when the players are in a slump, they'll replay tapes of past successes to remind the players of the thrill of achievement.

Here's a sweet experience from a mom who learned a valuable lesson about recording her best moments:

> Soon after my good friend was killed in a car accident, something was found among her possessions that changed my life. It was an insignificant-looking notebook that she called her "Happiness Is" book. Every day, she took note of the small blessings she noticed in her life and jotted them down.
>
> She recognized things like "a day at the park with my kids," "ham and crackers and macaroni and cheese on the floor all day, because not only does it mean I had a full and busy day, but that I have a baby to love," and "talking to Sarah on the phone" as

225

things that brought happiness to her life. (Imagine my thrill when I realized I had made someone else's happiness book!)

I determined to make one of my own, in memory of her. And I did. And I wrote in it . . . for a few months. And then I forgot all about it.

A few years later, I had just had my fourth child and was going through post-partum depression for the first time. After several months of learning and growing in ways I wasn't sure I wanted to learn and grow, I was still struggling and looking for something—anything—that could help me. I thought back to my friend's "Happiness Is" book and decided to give it a try again. Every night before bed, I jotted down some blessings I recognized throughout the day.

Like I said, it changed my life, but not right away. It was weeks, and even months, before I looked back and realized that the small act of recognizing and writing down those few gifts each day allowed me to feel gratitude. Not only for the big things — family, faith, a home, living in a free country; but also for the small things — a hot shower in the morning, the joy of watching a five-year-old discover his first loose tooth, a few free minutes to read a favorite book, and a husband who listens.

Taking a few minutes to write at the end of each day gave me something to look forward to. Soon I began to recognize little blessings as they occurred, and I felt consistent gratitude permeate my life. Two years later, I feel greater optimism and opportunity in my life than I ever have. Did having a "Happiness Is" list change everything? Perhaps not my circumstances, but it did change me.

- Sarah Bradshaw

I love that last sentiment. Recognizing, sharing, and recording the happiest parts of our days won't change the sequence of events, but they *will* change us.

Remember: Crisis + Time = Humor

We had three children very close, and one summer when they were four, two, and one, we were living in an extremely tiny apartment. Keeping our nap times in tact was of the utmost importance, and I'm sure you can imagine my angst when I heard my four-year-old coaching her two-year-old sister on how to "escape" from the crib: "Now Gracie, all you have to do is put one leg over like *this*. . . ." It absolutely wasn't funny at the time, when I was barely keeping things together, but looking back, that image always makes me giggle.

Around that same time, one of my friends was pretty upset when her four-year-old son colored in ballpoint pen all over their light-colored couch. In response to his mother's anger, he calmly replied, "Some parents *thank* their children for coloring on the couch."

One of my children's favorite stories is called "Hot Dogs and Peas." They beg me to tell it whenever we're folding laundry or cleaning the kitchen together. It all started when four-year-old Alia asked if she could leave the table to go play with her toys. I was on a business call, and I whispered, "First you have to finish your hot dogs and peas."

A few minutes later, she showed me her empty plate, and I nodded that she could go play. Then I looked over at Ethan in the high chair, and he had a *huge* pile of hot dogs and peas on his tray. I called Alia over, told her I'd discovered her little trick, and sent her to her room to sit on her bed. I tried to finish the phone call, but Alia was screaming at the top of her lungs about how unfair it was for her to be punished for "sharing" with Ethan.

Once Ethan finished picking his dinner off the mountain of food, I settled him into the bathtub with his sister, trying to keep the phone balanced on my shoulder and occasionally whispering, "Shhhhhhh" to Alia, who was still screaming as she poked her nose through a little crack in her bedroom door.

Two-year-old Grace finished up her bath first, so I dried her off and let her run naked into her bedroom while I scrubbed the ketchup off Ethan's face. Within seconds, Grace started shrieking (in tandem with Alia), and when I looked across the hall, I could see she'd had an accident on her carpet and she wanted me to clean it up *right that minute.*

I pulled the plug in Ethan's bath and let him play with the bath toys for a second while I went into Grace's room to pick up the mess on her carpet. I was only gone for 30 seconds, but Ethan decided he wanted to get out of the bath by himself (for the first time), and he dove head first over the edge of the tub, slipping onto the tile and crying for me to come pick him up. I was still on the phone at this point (what was I *thinking?*), and Alia's shrieks were simply getting louder, so I finally finished the call, wrapped Ethan in a towel, got a diaper on Grace, cleaned up the carpet, and sat down to talk with Alia.

Right then, my husband got home from school, and seeing me sitting so calmly with three happy children said with a smile, "How was your day?"

We've got a whole slew of stories like this, and when we review these "crises" as a family, we always end up laughing. The secret really is to learn to laugh now. I know this isn't easy, but remember, optimism is a skill. It's like learning to play Mozart. When you find yourself in a frustrating situation, ask yourself, "Will this *ever* be funny?" It usually will, and life just feels better when you're laughing.

Pay Attention to Who You're Becoming

Our work and sacrifice yield results—we just need to identify them.

As a first-time mom, I had all the same worries that any other first-time mom has. Will I be able to tell what my child needs and when? Will my child be healthy? Will I be comfortable nursing in public, or nursing at all? Will I ever be able to get back to that pre-mom shape?! My head flooded with questions that multiplied by the hour.

After ten years of motherhood, I feel confident in my ability to know what my children need and when they need it. We survived nursing, and it was almost a breeze. We even survived fourth grade, and at times, it was questionable with all of the drama. My husband and I have been able to conquer many experiences and are now proudly raising two very happy, outgoing, smart little girls, but it is the last question of getting back my figure that still seems to have gone unanswered.

As I think back to what my figure was in high school (when my high-school sweetheart—now husband—and I first met), I wonder why I didn't relish the cheerleading days of jumping, flexibility, and eating anything without gaining an ounce. With the new metabolism that graciously protrudes itself around my mid-section; I can't help but feel that those skinny days were just a dream. While I have tried many diets, quit drinking soda, and squeezed in various exercise regimes between work, sports and school activities for my kids, the weight seems to cling to me as much as my kids do when they are sick.

So, instead of focusing further on the weight, I propose a new way of looking at what I have "gained":

- *I have gained a wonderful daughter who looks more and more like me everyday, and who has taught me to be creative and look at the world in an entirely new way. She is growing up way too fast.*

- *I have gained a second amazing daughter who makes me laugh on a regular basis and who, for the moment, loves her mom terribly and wants to do everything she does. I know I'll miss these days when they go.*

- *I have gained the admiration of my husband who does remember to tell me how much he loves me and what a great mom I am when I am having a frazzled day and am fighting to balance work, homework and housework.*

- *I have also gained admiration for my husband, who, before our daughters were born, would not dance in front of anyone. He adores our daughters and has taught them to cook, fish, build a campfire, hunt and so many things that would fill a separate story. His support and involvement in their lives will make them well-rounded young women.*

- *I have gained a sense of pride at how happy our little family is, and I wonder in amazement (and worry at times) at what our girls will say and do next.*

- *I have gained patience that I never knew was possible. Food dumped on the carpet? No problem—that's why we have puppy dogs. Crayon pictures on the wall? Well, I guess we did need a little redecorating.*

- *I have gained a new kind of love that every new mother gains. It's not the kind of love you have for your husband, your parents or your siblings. It's a protective kind of love where you would do anything to keep this little person happy, safe, and healthy while still wanting them to make their own mistakes in order for them to grow.*

So, while I may have gained a little around the middle, I have also gained many wonderful emotions and memories that take my mind away from the fact that my stomach is now and forever lined with shiny stretch marks. To that, I say . . . "Go Figure?!"

- Chantól Sego

Developing that kind of optimism is a beautiful goal. Sometimes, though, it's hard to keep that perspective. At one point in my mothering experience, I felt like I was running on a hamster wheel. The housework was never "done," the writing I pored over each Wednesday evening wasn't getting published anywhere, and I wondered if my children were hearing *anything* I was saying to them.

One morning, I wrote this question on a half-sheet of paper: "What are we becoming today?"

I taped the paper to our refrigerator door, and then I mentally answered that question whenever I started feeling frustrated. When I wanted to yell at my boys for hitting each other with light sabers, but didn't, I realized that I was becoming more patient. When I sorted through the stacks of graded papers in my children's backpacks, I saw how they were becoming more skilled in math, writing, and science. When we gathered around the kitchen counter to decorate homemade scones with powdered sugar, I watched our family members laugh together, and I noticed that we were becoming closer friends.

Every single day, we are becoming *something*. Realizing that, growth can't help but inspire optimism.

Gain Control over Your Internal Voice

Every mother I know has an internal voice that sometimes gets out of control. Sometimes that voice says, "I am terrible. My life isn't

231

even that hard, and I still can't pull it together." To that voice, I say, "*Every* life has its hard parts, and I *will* pull it together."

Sometimes that voice says, "It's only 7 a.m. and I'm already in a bad mood. Guess today's going to be long and hard." A possible response? "Today might be hard, but that's okay. It's still going to be great. I can do this."

How about this one? "I look terrible. I don't even want to look in a mirror." A new friend recently taught me to say, "When I look in the mirror, I think, 'I bet I look at least 25 percent better to other people.'" That one made me laugh.

I've also heard my internal voice say things like, "I don't have the potential to live the life of my dreams. I just wasn't made to succeed." *That* voice is the trickiest. I used to listen to it every day—when I would decide not to exercise because I would "never look as toned as my muscular friends," or when I wouldn't even *try* to submit my writing for publication because I was "just a mom." Now I tell that voice that I have the potential to do exactly what I'm meant to do, and I will pursue those dreams with everything I've got.

Dance to the Music

Once there was a young boy who walked into a room where an older man wearing head phones was dancing like crazy. It was almost embarrassing to watch as he waved his arms, bounced his knees and moved his body with incredible enthusiasm. The young boy noticed a second set of head phones in the room, so he put them on and then shook his arms, bounced his knees and tried to do everything *exactly* like this man who was clearly enjoying himself. After a few minutes, however, the boy got tired—and a little disgusted—and he threw the head phones onto the ground and stomped out the door. What was wrong?

He hadn't turned on the music.

Have *we* turned on the music of motherhood? Do we see how fun this really is? Can we feel the magnitude of our work? Do we know what a difference we are making in the lives of our children . . . and what a difference they are making in ours? Or are we simply exhausting ourselves as we do the mommy dance that all those "other moms" seem to enjoy?

I couldn't always say this, but now I genuinely *love* motherhood. I don't love it because it's simple. I love it because I hear the music and I am making it a priority to enjoy the dance.

Living with optimism is a spiritual process for me, more than anything else. I feel powers beyond my own ability—helping me to change my heart, get the support I need, and feel hope that things, no matter how hard they are, will get better. We're not alone in this. There's purpose in what we're doing. These days with our children are *beautiful* days. We're going to miss them terribly at some point, and once we "have it all together," we'll wish we could go back and do it one more time—this time not focusing so much on the delayed shower, the messy kitchen, or that negative voice in our head.

As in the opening paragraph of this chapter, I could create a long list of frustrating details *every single day*—no problem. However, that's not going to help anything. What *does* help is remembering that my life, my purpose, and my motherhood experiences are not about *me*.

As we make a conscious effort to see the beauty, humor and growth in the stories of our lives, we become women with the power to make real differences in the lives of others—and the people whose lives will be improved because of what we offer aren't concerned one tiny bit with the timing of our showers.

Shawni grew up with stars in her eyes about motherhood. She pined away for the day she would have dozens of perfectly primped children lined up in a row . . . all with names beginning with "M."

Shawni grew up and married her college sweetheart, Dave, who gave her those children she dreamed of having. Although she didn't get her dozens (and only one of their names starts with an "M"), she feels blessed beyond blessed to have five of her favorite people as her children . . . even when they are complete ragamuffins (which is often). Shawni has found so much joy in the journey of motherhood and loves to share that joy with others through her blog at 71toes.com.

Shawni's youngest child, Lucy, was born with a rare genetic syndrome that causes blindness. Although this diagnosis has been heart-wrenching in so many ways, Lucy has been an amazing blessing and has taught their family to appreciate the small things.

With writing as one of her biggest passions, Shawni and her mother co-authored a book called "A Mother's Book of Secrets." In 2011 she had the honor of being named the National Young Mother of the Year by American Mothers.

CHAPTER TWELVE

MOTHERHOOD IS WORTH IT
The Power of Moments

by Shawni Pothier

Life is made up of moments, big and small.

There are the grand ones, like the moment your sweetheart slips that ring on your finger or when you hear that glorious newborn cry following the struggle of birth.

There are the awful ones, like when you hear your son's arm-bone crack when he falls off his bike.

And there are the heart-wrenching ones that make time stop sharp as the doctor tells you your daughter has a rare syndrome that will change her life. As you try to take in the awful news, you wonder how you can stay standing as the world starts to spin around you.

There are the thankless moments that encompass the minutia of motherhood:

- Listening to our children bluntly report that what we've painstakingly made for dinner is gross.
- Wiping up throw up.

- Picking up hundreds of random objects strewn about the house over, and over, and over again.
- Scrubbing ballpoint pen off couches.
- Wiping fingerprints from walls.
- Having teenagers talk back.

But that's not what this chapter is about.

This chapter is about the moments of motherhood that make it great. It's about those magical moments that swell in your heart and somehow make all the other tough and worrisome moments shrink in their wake. I'm talking about the moments where the air turns thick with love and your heart turns to mush.

Now, please note that the moments I'm talking about are not the perfect ones where everyone is dressed and clean with good manners abounding. They aren't usually the ones that are planned out or even anticipated. Instead, they are those moments that tend to hit unexpectedly. They are the ones that make you wish you had a camera attached to your hip, but since you don't, you try to memorize the details.

I am a photographer, which means I have pictures of practically every moment of my children's lives. But some of my most vivid "moments" are cataloged only in my heart: My son calling from his friend's house to tell me to look at the sunset. The entire-face-encompassing smile stretched across my daughter's face as we raced our bikes through the neighborhood one day in the fall . . . crunchy leaves swirling around as a backdrop. Sitting at a fast-food picnic table on a road trip and noticing how the sun slant makes my ragamuffin children appear to have halos.

Yes, some moments you can only capture with your heart.

Those are the moments that make up the magic of motherhood. Those are the ones we must let seep into our hearts and wash over the inevitable frustrations that also come along with the job.

The problem is that we have to stop long enough to notice these moments. Sometimes they tend to be embedded in the day-to-day chaos.

Sometimes they quite simply *are* the chaos.

There was a day a couple months ago where I actually started writing down the "moments" as they rolled on in front of me because my "moment" was realizing that wow, life is nuts.

Let's start by setting the stage:

> All five of my children are home from school . . . all of them with at least one friend traipsing through the kitchen while I cook dinner for us and for a sick pregnant friend to whom I offered to bring dinner two nights ago but forgot.
>
> The phone is ringing off the hook.
>
> Even if I wanted to answer the phone (which I don't), I would never be able to find the darn thing because our family has a knack for leaving those cordless things in the wackiest places. (The freezer? The pantry? Yep, I've found it there . . . and the sad thing is that I'm just a guilty as the rest of them.)
>
> My six-year-old is a broken record begging me to help her scrounge up some old fabric scraps so she can decorate a turkey drawing she's supposed to glam up for a school project. I keep promising I'll do it as soon as I get dinner in the oven.

237

I find my cell phone when it alerts me to a text, followed by some sort of important phone call, and as soon as I answer, I have three children suction-cupped to my side thinking that NOW is the time to talk to me about their day.

My twelve-year-old is getting ready for tennis and needs something to eat before she goes but is teary-eyed because she's in so much pain from her new elastics the orthodontist stuck on today. I stop and pull out the blender frantically throwing together a smoothie before her carpool comes.

The volleyball carpool has just called saying they have pneumonia and can't drive tonight when I'm supposed to be at book club.

My husband's 40th birthday is coming up, and my mind is partially wrapped around the phone conversation I had earlier with my friend who's husband is also turning 40 and the surprise party we need to get out invites for as soon as possible.

My thirteen-year-old is plunking hard on the piano because he's mad (again) that I won't let him quit piano lessons. And he can NOT seem to get that section of that song he's playing right. My heart sinks because I need to be in there helping him, but I need to be in here too or the sauce will burn, (and I need to be three other places too).

The seven-year-old and her friend (having given up on decorating the turkey) run in from the trampoline screaming because they have found there is a dead bee, of all things, in my daughter's hair.

All this is set to the music of my feisty four-year-old in one of her awful moods screaming for milk every time I turn around.

And just as the chaos reaches the peak of it's cacophony of noise my phone dings politely with a text from my dear husband reminding me I need to go vote. Let's note here that the voting booth closes in ten minutes.

Sometimes it takes a single moment like that to make you stop and realize how silly it is to be frantically chasing your tail and not really accomplishing anything. For some reason, that text on that day last fall amid the swirl of activity was my "moment." I don't know why, but it made me stop and almost laugh at the prospect of loading up all the kids in the car and rushing over to vote, picturing the guy there closing up the booth saying, "Sorry ma'am, you just missed your chance."

For some reason it made me stop and soak in the fact that I was there. Right where I needed to be. Not necessarily getting to everything I wanted to, but I was there, corralling chaos. My list of "to dos" would get done eventually. The world would go on if I didn't get my son to volleyball for one night. It would be okay even if I did burn the sauce and had to throw some Top Ramen on the stove instead. What was important was that I was *there*. And I was trying my best. I stopped right there to memorize everything around me because it hit me that my lists and "to dos" will always be there. But this precious afternoon with my children would disappear and meld slowly into another day . . . another set of worries and things to do.

Yes, sometimes the moments that fill up a mother's day don't seem to be so sweet. But if we step back and stop taking it all quite so seriously, we realize that life is good. So very good. And that brings the sweetness into the memories of even the craziest of moments.

I love this quote about interruptions:

"When you are exasperated by interruptions, try to remember that their very frequency may indicate the value of your life. Only people who are full of help and strength are burdened by other persons' needs. The interruptions which we chafe at are the credentials of our indispensability. The greatest condemnation that anybody could incur— and it is a danger to guard against—is to be so independent, so unhelpful, that nobody ever interrupts us, and we are left comfortably alone." - Anonymous (from *The Anglican Digest*)

I guess those interruptions to what could otherwise be sweet moments can *be* our "moments" as well. And it all works together to make up the beautiful tapestry of motherhood we are weaving day-by-day, crazy minute by crazy minute.

Stop Long Enough to Notice the Moments

A few weeks ago I read an interesting article about how tiring and burdensome motherhood is. Other mothers had made comments on the article in full accord. They complained of the mundane, dreary parts of motherhood.

I felt sorry for those mothers. Have I not felt the same way? Sure, motherhood is tough, there's no doubt about that. There are moments of pure mayhem when you think you just might explode if one more person needs your attention or one more "thing" is strewn around the house. But I felt sorry for those mothers because I realized in order to feel the way they were feeling, they must have forgotten to stop for long enough to soak in the moments. I know those moments were inevitably there . . . they always are in motherhood. But these complaining moms simply hadn't noticed them. They hadn't let those velvet moments wash away the abrasiveness of it all. They had forgotten to pause in the eye of their storms.

We all forget at times.

But if we can just train ourselves to stop and remember, how much happier we will be!

I love these thoughts:

> *"Being There [is] an emotional and spiritual shift, of succumbing to Being Where You Are When You Are, and Being There as much as possible. Its about crouching on the floor and getting delirious over the praying mantis your son just caught instead of perusing a fax or filling the dishwasher while he is yelling for your attention and you distractedly say over your shoulder: 'Oh, honey, isn't that a pretty bug.' It's about being attuned enough to notice when your kid's eyes shine so you can make your eyes shine back." - Iris Krasnow*

This is all good in theory. I mean, "being there" has been my mantra for years. I continually tell myself to slow down and make my eyes shine back at my children when theirs are sparkling at me. But just having good intentions doesn't necessarily do the trick, especially when driving five carpools, trying to help with four sets of homework, and still getting kids in bed at a decent hour. We must train ourselves to stop every now and then and soak in what is ours.

Sometimes I tend to think, "As soon as I'm done with _____, then things will run smoothly. As soon as I finish my responsibilities doing _____, then I'll be happy. Then I'll have time to skip off into the sunset enjoying my family."

But you know what? Life doesn't work like that. Things are never going to be "done." I'll never be all the way caught up. Sure, I can get more organized. I can implement new systems. But even after my big house-clean-out-mind-organization, there will still be another deadline. There will always be papers that need filing and emails that need replies. Fingernails will still need to be clipped. The toilets will still need scrubbing. All my children will still try to talk

241

to me at the same time, inevitably while I'm on the phone, and there will still be forty-five things pulling me in every direction.

But if we just remember that it's okay to stop and notice the "moments," we will really begin to enjoy this journey of Motherhood.

All these thoughts were brought into focus by an incident I had a little while ago.

It was an ordinary evening at our house and I was putting the girls to bed.

I was bugged.

It had been a long day. I was tired. I was achy. And I was ready for my children to drift off into sweet slumber.

I told them to brush their teeth.

They giggled and wrestled.

I begged them to put their pajamas on.

They formed a dog-pile on my nine-year-old's bed.

I knelt down for prayers in a huff, ready to launch into a lecture about how late it was and how we MUST get to bed.

But as I looked over at them all in a huddle of laughter and smiles— feet, arms, and straggly hair going every which way—something clicked inside me.

I forgot my achy tired-ness and filled up with still-ness and love for that moment in time—those three sweet girls froze time still for just a moment, all bunched up on the bed together. And I stood still long enough to memorize them in my mind.

Sometimes I forget to cherish the "doing," and instead I worry too much about the "getting it done." I wanted another thing on my mile-long list checked off. Of course, there were things that needed to be done. But what was five extra minutes going to hurt?

So I joined them. My smile joining theirs.

I love the journey of motherhood itself. Life is about more than just getting to that summit at the end of the road. All the accomplishments in the world won't give us much joy if we don't appreciate and soak in all the minutia that got us there.

I just need to stop and remind myself of that every once in a while.

In my mind, there is nothing quite so good as to be a Mother (except to be a wife, but that is a chapter for another book). And I must cherish those moments that make up my Motherhood—the good ones, the wild and crazy ones, and the heart-melting ones— while they last. Because before I know it these children will grow up and go off to create their own stories, and I'll be left with just the memories of all those life-enriching "interruptions" echoing through my house. How I hope that by then I'll look back and feel that I cherished the moments enough!

* * * * *

Drinking Life

They tumbled out of the car, ice cream cones in hand, and raced down the hill to the playground. When sticky fingers were licked clean, the games began. Freeze tag, up and down the slide, on the swings, then off again.

Up above, under sprawling branches, we watched them play, smiling as their laughter wound its way up the hill. The sunset behind the trees and a cool night breeze ruffled the leaves and the wisps of hair falling out of my ponytail.

Later, we joined them, kicking off our shoes and racing through the grass until the darkness nearly swallowed us all. Our laughter joined with theirs as we darted here and there, just out of reach, then intentionally into each other's arms.

Drinking life.

****

Just past midnight, I settled onto the couch, just me and the baby. I hushed her hungry cries, stroking her cheek and reveled in the divine harmony of mother and child. It's magical, really, this life giving. For a brief moment, her eyes looked into mine—tired, but bright, and our souls spoke, forging our connection just a little tighter than before.

Together, she and me. Drinking life.

****

I live for them, these moments. When the heavens open up and I catch little glimpses of the bigger picture, the bigger purpose of all this that we do. Not always extraordinary, but profound in the impression they give, the imprints they leave on my heart. Would that I were never too busy, too plugged into the mundane, the unnecessary, to breathe, to revel, to drink of this, my life.

- Jenny Proctor

Memories Made in the Moment

One morning, my kids were acting crazy, running around the house while I finished the breakfast dishes. Their noise increased, so I went to find out what they were doing. I approached my bedroom and heard giggling in my closet. The door was shut, lights turned off, with the vacuum blaring inside. The frustrated mother in me would have yelled at them, scolded them for turning the vacuum on when they weren't using it, and forcing them out of my room. With the thought to live in the moment, I opened the door and surprisingly found myself laughing. My kids were huddled around the vacuum, making pictures with their hands on the ceiling. The light from the vacuum was helping them create shadows. They asked me to join them, so I sat down for a few minutes to play and made a memory with my kids.

You see mothers, *Life isn't about waiting for the storm to pass . . . it's about learning to dance in the rain.* So, let's enjoy life and "dance in the rain" with our children. Turn up the music and dance in the living room together. Cuddle on the couch with blankets and books to read family favorites. Dress up and make funny faces. Laugh and play games. Go for a walk and see the world through our children's eyes. Remember, the dishes and laundry can wait. The phone can take a message. The computer screen will still be there when we get back. However, childhood is fleeting and moments with our children are to be made now.

- **Mindy Henry**

Tuesday Was One of the Good Days

Tuesday was one of the good days. You know the ones? The days where you feel the magic of being a mom. Where for just a little while the laundry and dishes don't matter and the feel of your baby in your arms and the sunshine on your face stops time.

It was a beautiful day, the sun shining and birds chirping. I took Em outside for some fresh air and playtime. We wandered around the cul-de-sac while she discovered bugs and rocks, all the while jabbering in her little toddler voice.

We continued our walk and a moment later she stopped me rather urgently in front of the neighbor's lawn, handing me her egg-shaped purple sidewalk chalk that had hitched a ride in her little fist, and I drew a heart and a kitty because those are the shapes that always make her smile. Eventually we found our way back to our driveway where she ran across the grass toward the trampoline. I hoisted her up and was rewarded with one of her trademark grins that lit her face. We bounced and bounced while she laughed and squealed.

Then I lay back, and she climbed onto my stomach, laying her head on my chest. Soon, in her little binkie-hindered toddler voice, she started to sing "Tink-o . . .tink-o . . .tink-o . . ." I joined her and we sang "Twinkle Star" and "Itsy-bitsy Spider" over and over. Soon she had quieted to just humming, and then silence. In that moment, with my baby girl on my chest, both of us bouncing softly with the sun warming us, I wanted time to stop. I complain. I whine. I get tired of it all. But I do realize that this time is fleeting. My last baby is growing and I can't stop her. Too soon the moment was gone. She needed some lunch and a nap. The day moved on with chores, making dinner, bath time, etc. But that one moment has stayed with me ever since. I need to create more moments like it on a daily basis so that when the more mundane moments of motherhood start to crowd in, I can remember *that* magical moment in the sunshine and the feel of my baby in my arms.

- Misty Pidcock

Peace

If you would have happened by a moment ago, you would have found me soaking in silence and feeling amazement. I was making

246

my nightly rounds. Kissing little, sleeping heads and lingering to watch them sleep. Turning off lights and locking doors. But then instead of locking, I opened the last one and stepped outside into the cool, still night. Enjoying the feel of the air on my bare arms, neck and face I lay down on the driveway and turned my face to the moon. I marveled at it and the stars twinkling across that big, black night. As I lay there looking up, I felt a warm tear make its way down my cheek. Not because I was sad or overwhelmed or even afraid . . . but because I was at peace. Total and complete peace. My gratitude and joy was so full, I could not hold it back.

In a world with so much turmoil, I've never felt so far away from it within the walls of my own home. Life is crazy, kids scream, dishes build up, schedules are full. But it is my oasis.

As I looked out into that big, black sky tonight, instead of feeling small, I felt as if peace itself was filtering down through those moonbeams. What more can any of us ask for?

- Sarah Young

Saving the Fish

My husband and I arrived home from a viewing one evening, dressed in our "Sunday Best." Our seven-year-old son, Luke, greeted us in the garage. With his big toothless grin, he proudly showed us a five-gallon bucket containing six tiny fish that he had just caught during a fishing class.

Outside the garage, the skies were darkening, the wind was blowing, rain was coming, and lightning could be seen in the distance. All Luke wanted was to put the fish in his "Secret Fishing Spot." It is only a short ride on the trail behind our house, but carrying a five-gallon bucket full of water and trying to avoid lightening strikes, I knew we had a quick decision to make. My husband and I knew the fish would not survive in the bucket until morning.

Personally, I had no cares about the fish, but I didn't want to see the excited, toothless grin disappear. As I walked into the house, I heard my husband suggest keeping the fish in the bathtub for the night. I'm sure the toothless grin got even bigger at that point, but I very quickly, volunteered to go change my clothes and ride our bikes together over to the "Secret Fishing Spot."

Luke and I jumped on our bikes, with me balancing the five-gallon bucket filled with water and six fish. As I began pedaling fast, I hoped the lightning would subside for just a while. With the wind blowing the hood from my head and rain falling on us, Toothless Grin and I set out to save the fish.

There are no photographs to capture the memory. I wish there were. But perhaps instead, the Toothless Grin excitement will be a treasured 'picture' I will see forever in my mind. As my son and I pedaled as fast as we could to get back home, the wind and rain howled around us. It was fitting, that above the sound of the falling rain, I heard a little voice coming from the Toothless Grin pedaling quickly behind me say, "You're the best mom in the whole wide world."

It was a fleeting, inconsequential moment in the grand scheme of things. Yet it was a precious moment I hope neither of us ever forgets. I ignored the rain and imminent lightening; I ignored all the rational, safety concerns mothers typically have because of six fish. I didn't do it because the six fish mattered to me. I did it because they mattered to my son.

- **Tiffany Sowby**

CONCLUSION

Finishing a good book is like leaving a good friend. - William Feather

We hope you feel that way now that you've reached the end of *this* book, and we also hope you feel the love and camaraderie from your friends who have invested the time, energy, and heart to write it.

The great news is that the friends you've just made are waiting for you online at The Power of Moms. We've even created a special page just for you: www.powerofmoms.com/book. At this "gathering place for deliberate mothers," we have a vibrant, thriving community, and you're invited to gather with us for ongoing inspiration, ideas, and support.

Come enjoy articles, book summaries, videos, podcasts, and programs—and find out more about our Learning Circles and Power of Moms Retreats. You might even want to be an author, a coach, or a trainer who helps take this incredible resource to more moms (who'll be so glad to find what they've been looking for).

The vision of our organization is to enable every mother in every community to feel part of a larger whole—so she and her family can not only survive, but live deliberately and *thrive*.

What you do in your family is vital to society, and your experiences (past, present, and future) will enable you to strengthen your peers and the next generation of mothers. It is *together* that we change and strengthen the world. We are so excited to have you as a part of The Power of Moms. See you soon!

Saren and April

INDEX

Made in the USA
San Bernardino, CA
02 January 2013